DATE DUE

NIKOLAI

Also by WILLIAM C. FLETCHER

A Study in Survival

NIKOLAI

Portrait of a Dilemma

(by) William C. Fletcher

THE MACMILLAN COMPANY, *NEW YORK*

COLLIER-MACMILLAN LIMITED, *LONDON*

TO *A Happier Enigma*

Library of Congress Catalog Card Number: 68-13209

FIRST PRINTING

The Macmillan Company, New York
Collier-Macmillan Canada Ltd., Toronto, Ontario

Printed in the United States of America

Contents

Preface

IF ANY CREDIT is due for this book, it certainly belongs not to the author but to Dr. Roswell P. Barnes. It was Dr. Barnes who first alerted me to the real importance of the life of Metropolitan Nikolai of the Russian Orthodox Church. He was able to see what all of us with the slightest knowledge about Nikolai's career should have seen, that Nikolai was one of those rare personages who present, writ large, the dilemmas confronting not only all Russian Christians, but in one degree or another all modern men. Dr. Barnes encouraged me to return again to Nikolai for intensive study, and as the work grew and began to take form, he guided its direction with innumerable and invaluable suggestions. Indeed, if this study contains any insight into the deeper issues, any comprehension of the ethical and spiritual dilemmas that confronted Nikolai, then surely these are not the product of my poor intellect but grew out of countless hours of conversation with Dr. Barnes, as we sat before the fire and talked about Nikolai, the Church, man in today's world, and ourselves. I suppose I will never learn enough to express what I owe to these conversations; suffice it to say that this book, at least, is an attempt to reflect the debt I owe to Dr. Barnes.

During my research for this book I had the great pleasure and good fortune to talk with a large number of people, Russians as well as Westerners, who had insight into the problems surrounding Nikolai. Some were acquainted with Nikolai personally—indeed, some knew him very intimately. Others had augmented their personal knowledge with years of study and research. I owe a debt to each of them, and if I do not list their names here it is primarily because of a desire to respect the confidence they had in me, and, perhaps, to avoid embarrassing these men by associating their names with a modest effort of my own. For the places in which I have trespassed against the counsel of any of them, I apologize, for the study that follows seeks its own path and could not possibly have been forced into the procrustean beds of the many contradictory evaluations of Nikolai's life.

I owe a considerable debt of thanks to a large number of other individuals who directly contributed in one way or another to my efforts in this study. Dr. Paul B. Anderson, my mentor in this as in so many other endeavors, contributed a rich fund of insights from his long experience and vast knowledge of the Russian Church. Richard H. Marshall, Jr., and Bernhard Wilhelm, my associates, contributed signally, the latter with countless facts that were outside my meagre store of knowledge, and the former with his time-consuming, considerate reactions to the early stages of the manuscript. Mary Edwards, who bore the brunt of the thankless task of editing, contributed far beyond the call of duty. Finally, my own family—particularly my wife—helped me invaluably in this work by their many suggestions and criticisms, but even more in enduring my presence during this study.

If the strengths of this book are due almost entirely to those who counseled me, its weaknesses are not. The only aspects for which I feel I can justifiably take full credit are the errors of fact and interpretation—these are my own, and are in no wise attributable to anyone associated with me while this study was being prepared.

In retrospect, this has been a rather disturbing study for me. It is really too early—much too early—to attempt a biography of Nikolai. The insuperable lack of data is less important in this regard than the fact that Nikolai was on the cutting edge of some of the keenest problems of modern life, and we simply have not had sufficient time for reflection and acclimation to the times in which we live. But this is precisely why the story should be told now, why an interim attempt should be made, for the issues involved are too crucial and immediate to remain dormant. So what was planned as a biographical study has had to content itself with being a mere portrait, for it almost seems that the more one learns about Nikolai and the closer one gets to him, the less one knows him. The confident, easy judgments one began with dissolve into the swirling, enigmatic mists surrounding the man, and one ends—as this study ends—unable to find a firm, comprehensible, valid rationale for Nikolai on one side or the other. Nikolai remains an enigma.

I guess that if this is what this study gives to the reader, if he leaves the book with the feeling that the real Nikolai has slipped out of the grasp of neat categorization, it will be enough. The book will have accomplished its purpose.

WILLIAM C. FLETCHER

Versoix, Switzerland
January, 1968.

I

Introduction

METROPOLITAN NIKOLAI of Krutitskii and Kolomna was one of the most widely publicized clerics of the postwar Russian Orthodox Church. Books, pamphlets, and articles in praise of him poured forth in almost limitless quantity for fifteen years. Concurrently, Nikolai was one of the most roundly vilified of modern churchmen, the subject of massive distrust and suspicion. His activities were reported in microscopic detail, and the degree to which his public life was documented is without equal among the leaders of the Russian church since World War II.

Nevertheless, the man himself remains a mystery. Despite the publicity which surrounded his activity, the character, personality, and inner life of Nikolai are obscure and indeterminate. In part this is due to the highly emotional response, positive or negative, elicited by the issues of international politics in which he was involved. But in greater measure, the impenetrability of Nikolai arises from the contradictory dimensions of his public life as a churchman. On first analysis, his participation in the political life of the Soviet state and his work as a pastor of the Russian church seem quite incompatible, to such degree as to make it incredible that a single person, however subtle and complex his rationale of life, could combine these two opposing dimensions in himself.

Ever since the Communist accession to power in 1917, the Russian church has led a precarious existence. The ideology of communism contains a deep formal commitment to the eventual eradication of religion, and in its practice the Communist regime in Russia has repeatedly demonstrated its endorsement of that goal by employing the massive resources of the Soviet state against the church. The continued existence of the church has been based on a tenuous balance whereby the church has sought to demonstrate to the state that it can be of sufficient usefulness to the state to justify at least a postponement of its complete eradication. After World War II what appeared to be a bargaining situation existed, in which the church, in return for its cooperation with and support of political policies of the state, received limited concessions sufficient to allow its continued functioning within Soviet society.[1]

Nikolai was the chief focus of this bargaining situation. From his accession to prominence in World War II until he left office in 1960, the primary services rendered by the church were in the area of foreign policy, and Nikolai's position as head of the church's Department of External Relations thus placed him at the center of the delicate, precarious balance of church-state relations in the USSR.

The public life of Nikolai is one of the few points of access to the tensions under which the Russian church as a whole and the Russian Christian in particular must operate. A reasonably accurate picture of the demands of the Communist state may be drawn by examining the many places at which state policy and church activities were joined in Nikolai, and because of the wide publicity that surrounded these areas of his life, a relatively detailed record is available. More important in this regard are Nikolai's many published speeches and articles, which provide an individualized record of this important aspect of the life of the Russian church.

A vastly different picture emerges from the second major body of Nikolai's works, his sermons. These sermons, delivered in the course of Nikolai's ecclesiastical duties, reflect normal activities of the Russian pastor. If the motivation of Nikolai's works dealing with political themes is to be found in the points at which state policy coincided with his work as a church leader, the motivations and aspirations found in his sermons come from a far different source. The sermons deal with issues arising from the deep springs of the Christian faith, from the two millennia of Orthodox tradition and the ten centuries of the history of the Russian church. Seldom do they reflect the interests and issues of the Communist state. In large measure because Nikolai's position as a churchman was useful to the state, many of Nikolai's sermons were published, both as a regular feature of the *Journal of the Moscow Patriarchate* and in collections translated into many foreign languages.

Thus Nikolai's life is unique and of vast importance, for nowhere else are these opposing tendencies so amply documented. The briefest consideration of a Christian church that exercises its ministry in a society governed by a political party professing militant atheism would suggest that there must be tension. In Nikolai both these aspects of church life in the Soviet Union are documented, and because both of these seemingly contradictory demands are joined in the works of a single cleric, the areas of tension can be discerned in detail. Nikolai is the unique point at which this crucial problem may be approached and from which may be drawn some attempt to evaluate the success or failure of the way in which the Russian church and Nikolai responded to the challenge of communism.

Despite the masses of documentation surrounding Nikolai's public life, however, not enough is known about him to enable one to penetrate through to the man himself. It was his public life, not his private life, that was the subject of publicity. Memoirs, notes, and personal observations, whether by Nikolai himself or by his intimates, either do not exist or have not been made public to complement the mass of materials that detail his public life during his years of prominence. And of his life prior to World War II there is little information of any sort.

This is a crucial lack. Considering the complexities of the issues in which he was involved, it would be futile to expect to gain full understanding from records of his public life, however great their volume. It was an individual human being who took these issues upon himself, and it is in his reaction—his fate—as a man that the issues ultimately have to be understood.

This study will attempt to make cautious forays beyond the evidence in portraying Nikolai, in full knowledge that such trepidation is anathema to the scholar and at best unsatisfying to the merely curious who insists upon a manageable, neat package for his staple. Concerning certain periods of his life for which the evidence is inadequate or lacking altogether, this study will direct attention to background considerations for which there is no domumentary or even necessary connection with Nikolai other than a high degree of probability that such events influenced his life. These attempts to go beyond the evidence, however, should be recognized for what they are and should never be received (nor will they be presented) as more than likely possibilities. The picture of Nikolai that will emerge will necessarily be tentative and approximate. In all likelihood, this presentation will not be adequate for those who seek a biography of the man. But it can be hoped that the issues that molded his life will emerge with sufficient clarity to allow an understanding of these vital events in the life of the Christian and his church. Until that bright day when complete records may become available, there are but two possibilities in dealing with Nikolai: remain in ignorance because the data are not complete, or attempt to derive some understanding—be it partial at best—from what knowledge we do have. It is from the conviction that partial knowledge is better than ignorance that this study arises.

From one point of view, it would seem that Nikolai's years of leadership in the church were highly successful. The position of the Russian church when he departed from public life was incomparably better than it had been when he first rose to prominence. During the postwar years the number of open churches grew from a low of 4225 or less in 1941 to some 15,000 or 16,000 by 1960. Whereas the church had had no theological seminaries before, in 1960 it had eight seminaries and two theological academies, and after a lapse of a generation it once more was becoming possible to fill vacant positions with formally trained priests. The complete isolation of the prewar church had evaporated during the years that Nikolai was in charge of the Department of External Relations, and the church carried on a relatively vigorous international life, with many contacts with other Orthodox churches and with religious and nonreligious personages from abroad in the peace movement. Nikolai lived to see the contacts with the ecumenical movement, which had begun during his leadership in the church, come to fruition as the Russian Orthodox Church was accepted into membership in the World Council of Churches.

The most important index of the success of Nikolai's years in church leadership was the relative relaxation of state pressure against religion. Antireligious propaganda, although never totally lacking during these years, did not compare with the continuous propaganda of prewar years, either in volume or in acerbity. Antireligious education in schools and universities was seldom emphasized as an ideal of Soviet education. Fulfillment of Christian ceremonies for birth, marriage, and death was seldom restricted, and certainly there was a little repetition of the earlier practice of state support of secular ceremonies in competition with these church rites.

The legal restrictions curtailing church activities were not formally rescinded during this period, but they were honored, to a large extent, in the breach. The antireligious aspirations of communist ideology were generally ignored by the Party, and, with the exception of a brief outburst of antireligious agitation in 1954, never entered into the decrees and pronouncements of the Party leadership. The governmental Council for the Affairs of the Russian Orthodox Church often seemed as much concerned with assisting the church as it did with carrying out the antireligious policies inherent in the ideology, and its leader, Georgii G. Karpov, when compared with his successor, seemed almost a friend of the church rather than its enemy.

Harassment of the church was minimal during Nikolai's years, both in terms of acts of public ridicule, which occurred relatively infrequently, and in terms of petty administrative annoyances designed to make church life more difficult, which occurred only within narrowly prescribed limits. Priests had considerable opportunity to teach the faith to children, and religious upbringing of children did not subject the parents to sanctions or severe pressure.

Finally, the church was subject to little or none of the outright pressure against which it had been all but defenseless during the prewar period. No great campaigns to close churches were visible during the latter years of Nikolai's career in the church, and religious shrines operated relatively freely, attracting pilgrims in unrestricted numbers. There were few if any bishops or priests arrested on questionable charges, and for a layman to suffer imprisonment for his faith became most unusual—a marked contrast to what had become the normal situation before the war.

If these indices of the life of his church are the criteria by which Nikolai's career is judged, there is little question that his service to his church was an unqualified success. When compared with every other period since the accession of the Communists to power in 1917, these were almost years of tranquillity and peace for the church, a time when the Orthodox church had good possibilities, within limits, for carrying out a ministry to the Russian people. To the extent that Nikolai's work was instrumental in securing these relatively unhampered conditions, it was highly successful.

But if his career is evaluated from the point of view of what lasting benefits he won for his church, the picture is vastly different. Few of the concessions and conditions for church activity for which he had labored survived Nikolai, and, in most respects, his work was of little lasting benefit to the church in its relations with the state. Within the five years after his death, nearly all of the concessions he had won had vanished.

The years following Nikolai's departure from church leadership were marked by a vigorous antireligious campaign, whose implementation by the state was scarcely less (and in a few respects was more) energetic than the most violent of the prewar propaganda campaigns.[2] Antireligious publications poured forth in drastically increased number.[3] Massive efforts were expended to introduce atheism once again into the curriculum of every educational facility in the country, and considerable resources were devoted to training specialists in antireligious activities.[4] Secular rites of birth, marriage, and death were introduced throughout the Soviet Union, and great efforts were made to supplant religious ceremonies and festivals with competitive events devised by the state.[5] For the first time in almost a generation, mass media resumed antireligious propaganda as a staple and ubiquitous part of the effort to penetrate the society with Party-devised indoctrination.[6] To these revivals of prewar antireligious activities was added a vast and systematic application of the technique of individual work with believers, an attempt to augment the mass approaches with personal techniques of persuasion.[7]

Long-dormant laws restricting church activity were revived,[8] and a new law was introduced and widely invoked, levying severe penalties against a very broad range of activities.[9] The Council for the Affairs of the Orthodox Church was transformed into an agency for ensuring the church's strict observance of legal requirements,[10] and the institutional cohesion of the Russian Orthodox Church was gravely damaged by the transfer of ecclesiastical authority to lay councils in the local church.[11] Most ominous of all was the fact that the renewed antireligious campaign enjoyed public support from the highest levels of Party leadership.[12]

Harassment of the churches increased markedly as a variety of annoying procedures were used to hamper church activity.[13] Religious training of children was made exceedingly difficult by the introduction of rules prohibiting children from attending worship services,[14] while priests were denied the right to teach religion to children at all, even at the request of parents.[15] And the several cases in which Baptist and Pentecostal parents guilty of teaching religion to their children were denied parental rights and their children sent to state boarding schools were a disturbing omen for Orthodox and non-Orthodox alike.[16]

The church suffered grave injuries under the onslaught of direct, forcible measures against which it had no visible defense. Great numbers of churches were closed[17]: by 1962 the number of Russian Orthodox churches had decreased from between 15,000 and 16,000 in the late fifties to 11,500,[18] and by late 1963 the church had lost an estimated half of its parishes.[19] Many monasteries and major shrines were closed and others were subject to crippling interference by the state.[20] Of the eight seminaries operating when Nikolai departed from public life, only three were functioning five years later.[21] Many bishops and priests were arrested and sentenced to long terms of prison,[22] and others were summarily (and gratuitously) confined to mental hospitals and sanitariums in lieu of arrest.[23]

Thus Nikolai's service to the church was not at all successful in achieving lasting benefits. Five years after his service ended the church was approaching its precarious position of the thirties, and whatever benefits Nikolai may have hoped to secure by his work vanished almost overnight. By the criterion of lasting results achieved, Nikolai's career was an almost total failure.

The one exception was the area of foreign affairs. The foreign activities of the church increased dramatically after Nikolai's death. For the first time the church entered into full participation in the ecumenical movement. Pan-Orthodox activities were resumed, and tentative steps were made toward contact with Roman Catholics. With the development of the Christian Peace Conference at Prague the Russian church resumed activity in the peace movement on a scale rivaling and perhaps exceeding Nikolai's work in that area.

There was a crucial difference in its international activity, however. If in Nikolai's time the church's international activities had been of benefit to state interests and the state had reciprocated with concessions to the church within Russia, no such concessions were forthcoming from the expanded international activity of the church after Nikolai's death. What had seemed a bargaining situation during Nikolai's leadership of the church's foreign policy broke down after his death, and the state was able to enjoy whatever benefits it could reap from the church's foreign affairs without paying the hitherto accustomed price in concessions in return.[24]

The Russian Orthodox cleric who was in charge of these new ventures in international affairs was Metropolitan Nikodim. He had replaced Nikolai when the latter was relieved of his responsibilities as head of the church's Department of External Relations, and, very soon after the departure of Nikolai, Nikodim assumed his mantle as the leading Russian Orthodox cleric, second only to the patriarch.

Born in 1929, Boris Rotov abandoned his studies at the Riazan Teacher Training Institute to become a monk in 1947, taking Nikodim as his monastic name. Despite his lack of theological training, he was ordained to the priesthood in 1949 and spent the next six years serving first in a parish, then as a rural dean, and finally as secretary to the archbishop of Yaroslavl and Rostov. Concurrently, he completed in five years the twelve-year correspondence program of the Leningrad Theological Academy, and was awarded the degree of Candidate of Theology in 1955. His candidate's thesis was on the Russian mission at Jerusalem, and shortly thereafter he was sent to Jerusalem. He became head of the mission, in charge of all church affairs in Israel, in 1957.

In March 1959, now with the rank of archimandrite, Nikodim was recalled to Moscow, and in June he became the assistant to Metropolitan Nikolai in the Department of External Relations. One year later he replaced Nikolai as head of foreign affairs of the church, and was elevated to bishop. At thirty-one he was the youngest bishop in the Russian church since before the Revolution. In 1961 he was appointed Archbishop of Yaroslavl and Rostov, and in 1963, at the age of thirty-four, he became Metropolitan of Leningrad and Lagoda. Unquestionably, he was the most important, and probably the most powerful, bishop in the church next to the patriarch himself.[25]

This was a meteoric rise. So swift was Nikodim's climb to prominence that many have suggested that the state was responsible for it. Considering the lack of evidence, it would probably be an oversimplification to suggest that his elevation was accomplished by the state rather than by the church, and, in addition, this hypothesis runs the risk of ignoring his very considerable abilities; Nikodim is one of the most able men the Russian Orthodox episcopacy has produced in this century, speaking several languages and able to conduct conversations competently on any number of subjects, including complex and subtle theological matters. But by the same token, it would be unrealistic to think that his precipitate rise was contrary to the desires of the state.

The same was true, of course, of Nikolai. The position of chairman of the Department of External Relations is probably the most critical position in the Russian church, at least insofar as the state is concerned. If there is a point at which state use of the services of the church has its locus, it is in this person, for it has been in Soviet foreign policy that the regime's attempts to use the church in support of its policies have been most prominent. Thus the position requires a man of considerable ability, and, like Nikodim, Nikolai was one of the most talented bishops of the church. By the same token, however, the position requires a man who is acceptable to the state, and no less than Nikodim, Nikolai was able to make himself acceptable to the state, at least until shortly before his death.

Just as the work requires certain abilities in the man who is to fill this position, it may be that, because the position is caught in the often contradictory demands of the Communist state and the Christian church, there is a certain logic, a certain pattern of development operative on whoever it is that fills the position. It requires a high degree of skill to bridge the two fields of activity successfully, and not even the most able of men can be expected to join these contradictory directions with complete success: he must always seek a workable balance between the two directions, and inherent in the responsibilities of the office is the possibility that circumstances may come that will force him to choose the one or the other, finally and irrevocably.

Quite possibly this may have been what occurred in Nikolai's life. Nikolai's public career repeated with remarkable similarity that of his immediate predecessor, Metropolitan Sergii (Voskresenskii), for almost certainly Sergii's career led him to that point of final decision.

Metropolitan Sergii was the first to occupy the position of focal point between church and state. During the thirties he was apparently the chief mediator between the church and the state, and was roundly distrusted by the Russian

Orthodox people in Moscow as a mere Soviet agent. He was one of the four bishops to survive the decade of the thirties, in office, and was by far the most prominent next to the patriarchal *locum tenens*. With the partitioning of Poland in September 1939 and the conquest of the Baltic states shortly thereafter, Sergii was sent to the newly acquired areas in order to aid in the process of enforced sovietization. When the German invasion came two years later, he was in Riga, serving as patriarchal exarch.

Sergii apparently was quite accustomed to working in close collaboration with the Soviet Secret Police; indeed, in many ways he had built his career on his ability to get along with the emissaries of the state. Apparently he was considered by the populace in the newly acquired areas not only as the representative of the relatively weak church, but also, because of his access to the Secret Police, as a representative of no inconsiderable power as well.

When the Germans invaded, however, Sergii refused to evacuate with the Soviet government. He hid in the cellars of the cathedral to avoid the evacuation party that had been sent for him, and when the Germans arrived he welcomed them. Sergii spent the remainder of his life under the German occupation powers, contributing to the German propaganda against the Soviet regime by his personal revelations of the pressure that the church had suffered under the Communists. At no time did he renounce his allegiance to the Moscow patriarchate. Even when the interests of German propaganda required him to do so, he refused. It was apparently this refusal that cost him his life, for he was shot from ambush on April 29, 1944, apparently on the orders of the Germans. There is a lesser possibility that he was shot by the Communists, in which case it had been his refusal of the Soviet regime's order to evacuate that led to his death.

Aside from the very great personal motivations that might
have induced Sergii to renounce the Soviet government
during the invasion of Riga, there appears to be one over-
riding motivation that was quite unconnected with his personal considerations: the desire to serve the church. To judge
from his statement after his defection to the Germans, it
would seem that his chief motivation was the good of the
church. He felt that he could serve the church more effectively from behind the German lines than he could by
continuing his subservient relationship to the Soviet state
within Russia. The sincerity of this motivation was borne
out by his refusal to renounce allegiance to the patriarchate,
even when such refusal would cost him dearly.[26]

Thus, Sergii, the first to occupy the difficult position of
mediator between the interests of church and state in the
USSR, ended his life by choosing to serve the church,
despite the possibility (which proved to be actuality) that it
would cost him his life to do so. There is a curious parallel
between his life and that of Nikolai.

It is in Nikolai that the contradictory forces inherent in
the position are most clearly visible. In the mass of literature
produced by and about him one can find the tensions that
are the inevitable concomitant of the position of chairman
of the Department of External Relations. If one is to have
some insight into the peculiar tensions facing the Russian
Orthodox prelate who leads the church's foreign affairs, it
is obviously necessary to examine the life of Nikolai.

Less directly, Nikolai's career also yields a token of insight into the current position of religion in the USSR. That
the antireligious campaigns were muted from 1939 until
1960 was due in no small measure to the service he rendered
to his church by his service to the state, and the end of his
career not only coincided with, but to some degree may have

caused or been caused by, the beginning of the subsequent antireligious campaign.

There is a more profound reason for studying the life of Nikolai, however. In his life, as in no other focus, is documented the history of the Russian church since 1917. His career was formed by the events of that history, and from 1939 on he played a leading role in the major events in the history of his church. Nikolai was at the center of, and often personally responsible for, those events between 1939 and 1960 that determined the direction the church would take, not only in its foreign affairs, but also within Soviet society, and in particular, in its relations with and attitudes toward the ruling forces in that society. An understanding of Nikolai's life is an understanding of the modern history of the Russian church, not in the pedestrian terms of academic church history, but in the vital terms of one who lived and, as much as any man can, embodied that history. If insight into the inner dynamics, into the personal and subjective elements of a period is as important to the historian as the list of names, dates, facts, and figures, then a study of Nikolai's life promises to yield more in genuine understanding than would volumes of history texts.

There is a final reason to turn to Nikolai's life that, perhaps, outweighs all the others. Nikolai was a man of the twentieth century—witness, actor, and perhaps a victim of some of the sternest realities of this century. In him, as in no other, was written the full volume of the problems, pressures, temptations, and opportunities of a churchman in the first of the modern total states. If there is to be any understanding at all of what it means to be a Christian and a churchman in circumstances, societies, and environments like that of the Soviet Union, then Nikolai's life must be-

come one of the chief texts of modern Christian understanding.

And perhaps, in the sharp contrasts of Nikolai's life, there
lie the beginnings of an understanding of what it means to be
a Christian in any society, in any time, and in any place in
which a fallible individual finds himself confronted with a
world that has little time and little sympathy for a phenomenon that seems so impractical, so unrealistic, so fragile as
the Christian faith.

II

*Years of Background**

NIKOLAI COMPLETED his master's dissertation in 1917. The tsar had abdicated in February of that year, and in October the Provisional Government would fall to the Communists. The old order was dying, and Russia was about to enter into the modern, Soviet period. The end of Nikolai's formal education and his entrance into the active ministry of the Russian Orthodox Church thus coincided with the debut of the new era in Russia. Nikolai's career as a churchman was contemporaneous with the first forty-three years of the history of the Soviet Union.

Nikolai, then, was a modern Russian cleric. Although his family was solidly entrenched in the priestly caste of Russia, he did not receive the traditional education of a priest's son. Born Boris Dorofeevich Iarushevich on January 13,

---

* Biographical data on Nikolai may be found in V. Nikonov, "His Grace Nikolai, Metropolitan of Krutitskii and Kolomna," *Zhurnal Moskovskoi Patriarkhii*, April 1952, pp. 9–21. An analytic treatment may be found in Wassilij Alexeev, *Russian Orthodox Bishops in the Soviet Union, 1941–1953* (New York: Research Program on the USSR, 1954). A convenient outline biography is available in English in U.S., Congress, Senate, Committee on the Judiciary, *Communist Controls on Religious Activity* (Washington, D.C.: U.S. Government Printing Office, 1959), pp. 26–27.

1892, he was unable to attend the normal theological seminary for his secondary education because his father's parish
was too far from the nearest seminary. Instead, he attended
a secular gymnasium. Even though he had already decided
upon an ecclesiastical career, he then matriculated in the
St. Petersburg University's department of physics and mathe-
matics, for this would free him from the requirement of
taking the final two years of seminary training as prerequisite
to entering the Theological Academy.

In 1910 a change in the church rules allowed him to enter
the Academy directly. According to his almost hagiographic
biographer, V. Nikonov, four decades later, he was an exceedingly brilliant student:

> He attended the lectures punctually and conscientiously, he
> submitted his term papers on time, he took his course examina-
> tions without delay. Gifted with sparkling ability, he was notice-
> ably outstanding among his comrades, among whom there were
> able and hardworking people. But nevertheless it always turned
> out that the first in the course was B. D. Iarushevich. To com-
> pete with him seemed too daring and hopeless a matter. They
> competed for second and third place, but not for first, which
> was reserved for B. D. Iarushevich.[1]

While it would be prudent to retain a degree of reserve
regarding the paeans of praise in his official biography, there
is corroborating evidence that he was indeed extraordinarily
intelligent, gifted, and studious.[2] After graduation from the
Theological Academy, he decided against the academic
career to which his excellent work seemed to lead and chose
instead to embark on a career in the hierarchy of the church.
He took monastic orders on October 23, 1914, choosing as
his monastic name Nikolai. He was promoted from monk to
archdeacon the next day, and on October 25 was elevated to
hieromonk—an exceedingly swift rise, though not, perhaps,

unusual for one whose work at the academy had been so outstanding.

In 1915 Nikolai spent a short period as a chaplain in the Russian Army, but, for reasons not specified in his official biography, he did not complete his service and returned the same year to resume graduate work at the Petrograd Academy. He completed the two-year course with high honors, and at twenty-five was the youngest master in the academy's memory.

Nikolai's master's dissertation was entitled "Church Jurisprudence in Russia Prior to the Publication of the Conciliar Code of Aleksii Mikhailovich (1649)." This was an ambitious examination of a comparatively unknown subject requiring considerable original research and much familiarity with both ecclesiastical and secular law. Nikolai did a suprisingly good job of it. He had chosen the same topic for his candidate's (undergraduate) thesis, and received commendations and cash prizes for it both then and in its expanded form in 1917. While copies of the 666-page printed version are not available in the West, Nikonov quotes the following extract from the Introduction:

There is no denying that an analysis of church jurisprudence in the ancient ecumenical Church must serve as the point of departure for our analysis of church jurisprudence in the period of the first centuries of the life of the Russian Church and state. There the first principles of jurisprudence in general, and the first laws of ecclesiastical judicial order and judicial conduct were worked out, there the first procedural rules and the forms of juridical practice were developed. To the extent to which the Russian Church received her being from the Byzantine Church, and to the extent to which she should follow the example of her Mother in origins and conduct of her life, in the organization of her government and activity, to that extent it is essential for us to understand also the inner working of church jurisprudence in Byzantium. . . . What, in ancient Russian church jurisprudence, should be considered a result of ancient ecumenical legislation and practice, and what is a result of the independent conduct of the activity of the Russian state and the Russian Church, or in other words, on what ancient ecumenical bases was the active energy of Russian state and church thought based.[3]

From this brief extract it would appear that Nikolai's chief interest as an advanced student was the correct and exact interpretation and development of ecclesiastical law. His other major interests at this period were liturgics and homiletics, in which he was an instructor.

Among the articles he wrote as a student was one whose title was strangely prophetic: "The Emperor Decian's Persecution of Christians." The Russian church was soon to enter a period of great difficulty. Hopes for continuing governmental favor were finally ended with the Bolshevik coup d'état. Nikolai was working at an unspecified parish during the crucial events of the fall of 1917 and naturally took no part in the historic council, which, immediately after Lenin's accession to secular power, elected Russia's first patriarch since Peter the Great.[4]

In January 1918 the state began its campaign against the church, and the church answered the challenge with vehement defiance. The new government declared the separation of church and state, and Patriarch Tikhon replied with his first decree, excommunicating the Communists. The church continued its open resistance for at least a year, suffering resounding defeats in the face of the superior forces at the service of the state. Nikolai, however, as a young cleric, was not directly involved in the conduct of the struggle. In 1918 he was transferred to the Peter and Paul Cathedral in Peter-hof.

In 1919 Nikolai was appointed archimandrite in charge of the Alexander Nevsky Lavra (Monastery). It was also in 1919 that the Patriarch appears to have abandoned the policy of hostility to the Communists in favor of political neutrality, but this change probably did not help Nikolai. His was not a particularly comfortable post to occupy. The government would soon begin wholesale attacks on the Lavras, exposing relic frauds and other irregularities as a part of its propaganda campaign against the church. While the relic frauds would soon lose their novelty, the antireligious propaganda of the state would be a continuing factor in Nikolai's environment, waxing and waning in intensity for the next forty years.

Troubled times followed. Russia was embroiled in civil war, and large numbers of churchmen, accused of aiding the White armies, were summarily dispatched as counterrevolutionaries by the Red forces of the Bolshevik government. The Civil War ended in 1921, only to be followed by a disastrous famine, which the government employed with great effectiveness against the church. The government ordered church valuables to be confiscated to aid the hungry, and Patriarch Tikhon replied by willingly ordering that unconsecrated articles be donated, but called upon the churches to resist the confiscation of consecrated valuables. Bloody riots followed, and well over a thousand priests were arrested. Scores of bishops were also arrested, among them the popular Metropolitan Veniamin of Petrograd, who was tried and executed.

The depletion of the number of bishops tended to make advancement in the hierarchy of the church unusually swift, but this advantage for the younger clergymen was more than outweighed by the great risks involved in the episcopacy. Bishops were to be the primary focus of the state's hostility to the church, and additional exiles were constantly added to the large number of prelates imprisoned on the frozen island of Solovky in the far north as the state's campaign-against the church progressed. Nikolai was elevated to bishop of Peterhof, a vicarial see of the Petrograd archdiocese, on March 22, 1922.

Within two months of this time the Russian Orthodox Church was in schism. In an attempt to divide and further weaken the church, the state enthusiastically supported a group of liberal clerics, whose seizure of power began the famous Living Church Adventure. Patriarch Tikhon was imprisoned after he had agreed to give to the liberal clerics the duty of transferring the patriarchal archives to his appointed successor. His successor never arrived; the state refused to grant him permission to travel to Moscow.

The Living Church group proclaimed itself the successor to leadership in the Russian church, despite the exceedingly tenuous basis for such a claim from the point of view of canon law. The Living Church clerics, however, seemed little concerned with canonicity, for in the following months they forced through a series of sweeping reforms, some of which were in flagrant violation of the canons of Orthodoxy.

There was serious opposition to the reformers. Great masses of believers repudiated the Living Church because of the obvious collaboration of its leaders with atheistic rulers of the state. Even clerics not particularly hostile to collaboration with the Communist government, perhaps on grounds that the Byzantine system was a precedent, were greatly critical of the reform group's indifference to the canons of the church. This complete disregard for Orthodox laws and traditions would be felt especially keenly by those clerics who had extensive training in and a deep commitment to canon law.

Nevertheless, the Living Church grew rapidly, gaining control of most of the major cathedrals and important positions in a very few months. It was scarcely a secret that the Living Church owed the bulk of its success to the timely intervention of the Secret Police. Clerics who refused to accept the Living Church were quickly arrested, and were replaced by the Living Church with clerics of its own choosing. Nikolai was arrested in 1922, and was imprisoned until 1924.[5]

This was probably Nikolai's first intimate contact with the Soviet Secret Police. During the chaotic early days of the Civil War, the regime had formed the so-called Extraordinary Commission (Cheka), giving it broad, almost unlimited, powers in dealing with real or imagined counterrevolutionaries in the war zone. Under the exceedingly able, and ruthless, Felix Dzherzhinskii, the Secret Police grew into a truly formidable institution whose powers extended to all aspects of Soviet life. Despite its frequent change of name (Cheka, then GPU, NKVD, MVD, MGB, now KGB) it has retained its institutional continuity to the present day.

The Secret Police has traditionally been assigned the task of supervising religious activity. Originally, religious affairs appear to have been under the jurisdiction of the Commissariat of Justice, but the Secret Police quickly assumed this responsibility. It would appear that this arrangement continued even after two councils for religious affairs had been established under the Council of Ministers of the USSR in 1943 and 1944. Thus Nikolai's unhappy introduction to the Secret Police in 1922 marked the beginning of an aspect of his life as a churchman that in one degree or another would accompany him throughout his ecclesiastical career.[6]

Nikolai was released from prison in 1924. The opinion has been widely held that, at least in the prewar period, it was all but impossible for clerics to gain their release from confinement without submitting to the demands of the state. As long as they continued in that attitude of noncooperation that led to their arrest, they had no hope of release. According to one *émigré* priest who himself was imprisoned on Solovky in the twenties:

The whole clergy passed through a notorious filter and could not be delivered from prison and exile without compromise (if the authorities still offered it). All were regulated by repression. Of the unwilling remainder of the old bishops, to say nothing of the new, all were in prisons and did not receive freedom gratis. . . .

If terror has such a huge influence on the conduct of the Moscow Patriarch, then it is vain to speak about consideration of the Church's profit and to see in this wisdom, politics, gain, hope. Nothing of the sort. All of its positions are not sold, but are given away, as a man gives them away who signs his personal death sentence. He is informed about the sentence and he signs what he reads. If he remains yet alive, then he lives each day on the mercy of his conqueror and does everything which is ordered. He works like a slave doomed to death, who has had everything taken out of his soul and for whom there is no case at all for morality and shame. It has all long since been destroyed. The death sentence may be executed and fulfilled on any day. Work for each day. . . .

Thus, we undoubtedly have before us people who have fallen in the time of persecution, who, under the threat of death, bring sacrifices to the new Soviet idols.[7]

According to this line of reasoning, then, Nikolai must have purchased his freedom by capitulating to the demands of the state, becoming, in effect, an agent of the Secret Police from that time on.

However, this view may not be entirely correct, at least not in every case. During the years of Nikolai's imprisonment, 1922–24, the Soviet forced-labor system had not yet been developed.[8] By comparison with conditions after 1927, the regime in the exile camps was quite lenient. Inasmuch as the Soviet government had not yet come to rely heavily on the economic fruits of the forced-labor system, there would be less reason for arbitrary extension of a prison term in these early years, and thus it might be possible that the price of full capitulation was not exacted of every cleric who completed his prison term.

In Nikolai's case, it would not appear that he had been required to make a full recantation of the specific issue that had led to his original arrest, his refusal to accept the leadership of the Living Church. Although Patriarch Tikhon had been released in 1923 and the magnetism of his image as patriarch had begun the defeat of the schism, the regime was not to become disenchanted with its creation until 1925 at the earliest. In 1924 the Living Church still enjoyed the support of the state. Yet there is no evidence that Nikolai at any time modified his rejection of the Living Church. Thus it seems unlikely that he bought his freedom by recanting his specific offence, although this in itself does not necessarily militate against cooperation with the Secret Police in some less obvious manner.

In 1925 Patriarch Tikhon died, and with him died the church's policy toward the state that he had embraced in 1919. Political neutrality on the church's part was no longer acceptable to the state. After Tikhon's release from prison the state had appeared to be content with his neutral position, but immediately after his death his successors were quickly arrested, one by one, until there remained only Metropolitan Sergii (Stragorodskii), third in line to succeed the third of Tikhon's designated successors. Even though Sergii proclaimed again the policy of political neutrality in 1926, he was soon arrested himself. With his arrest the central authority in the church was in grave danger of complete dissolution, and it was plain that political neutrality would not protect the church leadership against arrest.

Nikolai doubtless was keenly interested and much disturbed by the drama unfolding in the succession crisis following the Patriarch's death. With his interest in canonicity, he could not have been unconcerned about the troubles befalling his church, for the valid succession of central authority is one of the keystones of canonical validity for an Orthodox church.

He does not appear to have been directly affected by the state's attack on the central hierarchy, however. The state's chief interest from 1925 to 1927 seems to have been directed to the leadership of the institutional church, and no general attack against the church at large seems to have been resumed until 1928.

In 1927 Sergii, imprisoned for the third time, was released, and almost immediately the official state newspaper, *Izvestiia*, published his proclamation of July 1927. In this proclamation Sergii in effect repudiated Patriarch Tikhon's policy of political neutrality, which was manifestly unsuccessful in gaining for the church a *modus vivendi* in the new society, and replaced it with a new policy of active political support for the Communist state, regardless of the fact that its leaders proclaimed themselves atheists. The crucial section of the proclamation was as follows:

We wish to be Orthodox and at the same time to claim the Soviet Union as our civil motherland, the joys and successes of which are our joys and successes, the misfortunes of which are our misfortunes. Every blow directed against the Union, be it war, boycott, or simply murder from behind a corner . . . we acknowledge as a blow directed against us. Remaining Orthodox, we remember our duty to be citizens of the Union "not from fear, but from conscience," as the Apostle has taught us (Rom. 13:5).[9]

Sergii's new course was a carefully delimited policy; he offered to the state the full, active support of the church, but that was all. His change of policy was a change of political policy only, and, unlike the Living Church reformers, he did not allow for changes in any other area of church life; the canonical, dogmatic, and liturgical life of the church was to remain inviolate.

Even in its promise of political support, the proclamation made a small, but exceedingly important, distinction. While the distinction is difficult to find in English translation, the Russian grammatical construction of the crucial paragraph makes it clear that the church recognized the Soviet Union as the motherland, but it was the joys and successes of the motherland with which the church identified itself. This subtle distinction left an opening whereby the church need not support those activities that might be considered "joys and successes" by the regime but that might, according to the church, be detrimental to the motherland—activities such as the growth of atheism in society, which, despite the proclamation, has never received a word of support from the church.

The most important factor of the change in policy in 1927 would become apparent only after more than a decade. The new policy, because it offered to the state the political collaboration of the church, made it possible for the church to negotiate with the regime. In return for its support in specific political projects, the church could seek concessions in return, such as the permission to maintain a limited number of active churches and to conduct other activities necessary to its continuing functioning within Soviet society. While this possibility of gaining concessions was foreseen by Sergii in 1927, it was not until World War II that the policy bore fruit for the church. The church's continued activity within the postwar Soviet Union was a direct result of this bargaining position undertaken by the church in 1927. And from the war onwards, Nikolai would be the chief actor in the negotiated settlement with the state.

What Nikolai's personal reactions to the change in policy were in 1927, of course, is unknown, but events were quickly to demonstrate that he did not find the new political position objectionable. A great many Russian churchmen, however, were scandalized by the proclamation. A storm of protest arose. There were riots in Moscow, and great numbers of believers left the patriarchal churches, choosing the insecurity of illegal gatherings rather than submit to compromise with the atheists. Leningrad became one of the chief centers of the protest, since its Metropolitan, Joseph, in consequence of the proclamation, refused to submit to Sergii's order transferring him away from Leningrad, and so became the leader of an underground church, which spread widely throughout the USSR and caused the Secret Police no end of difficulty before it was finally disrupted in the early thirties.

The Josephite schism, however tragic it might have been for the unity of the church, was very beneficial to Nikolai's career. Because he accepted the leadership of Sergii (which, of course, implied acceptance of Sergii's political policy toward the government), Nikolai was one of the few bishops left in the archdiocese and, according to Nikonov, he and Aleksii (Simanskii), the future patriarch, were given the task of administering the Leningrad archdiocese. Aleksii, who was several years Nikolai's senior, was soon called to membership in the synod that Sergii had formed, so Nikolai appears to have inherited the archdiocese, even though at the time he was only a vicarial bishop. The Josephite schism thus left Nikolai in charge of one of the largest and most important positions in the Russian Orthodox Church, and his advancement thereafter could be expected to be swift indeed.

Unfortunately, conditions were most unfavorable for advancement in the hierarchy of the church. In 1928 the state undertook a rapid campaign of forced industrialization and collectivization of the peasantry, and the chaos that ensued at times seemed close to the brink of civil war. Concurrently the state unleashed a truly vicious attack on religion. Hundreds of bishops, thousands of priests, and countless laymen were arrested in the next four years, joining the burgeoning ranks of the forced-labor system. Thousands of churches were closed, and communication with the central authorities of the church became nonexistent for most dioceses. Bishops such as Nikolai, so long as they remained at large, generally had to administer their dioceses independently without any contact with the central administration of the church.

The antireligious campaign began to slacken late in 1932, and although atheistic propaganda continued to flood the country and the ubiquitous Secret Police were never far away, conditions were moderated somewhat during the next four years. In 1935 Nikolai was elevated to Archbishop of Peterhof. It was also in 1935 that Sergii was forced to disband his Synod, which returned Aleksii to the administrative duties of the archdiocese of Leningrad. It is not impossible that Nikolai was promoted in order to ensure that Aleksii's return to the administration of Leningrad, over which Nikolai had apparently been exercising almost independent jurisdiction, would not be misinterpreted as a demotion for Nikolai.

In 1936 Nikolai was made archbishop of the Novgorod and Pskov archdioceses, a position which he occupied until 1940. According to Nikonov:

> The patriarchal *locum tenens*, Metropolitan Sergii, often had the intention of transferring Bishop (and then Archbishop) of Peterhof Nikolai to a higher archepiscopal see, but such intentions were followed by energetic "rejections" on the part of the Peterhof and Leningrad flock. Delegations were sent from the believers to Moscow, and the flock kept its beloved arch-pastor.[10]

This may be true. However, it seems much more probable that during most of the period in question Metropolitan Sergii seldom had more than sketchy knowledge of Nikolai and his activities, and that the believers had more worrisome matters on their minds than sending delegations to Moscow.

The relative calm of the mid-thirties was soon to be shattered by a new attack on religion. Stalin was building toward the Great Purges, and in 1936 the church became caught up in the storm of accusations, arrests, and executions. The antireligious attacks of 1936–38 were the worst that the church had experienced, judging by their effects. The church was left prostrate by the purges: it was reduced to 4,225 open parishes by official figures and, according to some independent estimates, less than one-fourth of that number were actually functioning. The toll on the episcopacy was especially severe: at least fifty bishops are known to have perished during the purge years, and there were great numbers arrested on charges of espionage. By the end of the Great Purges the entire active espiscopacy of the Russian Orthodox Church consisted of just four bishops: Sergii (Stragorodskii), who was the patriarchal *locum tenens*, Sergii (Voskresenskii), Aleksii, and Nikolai. All the other bishops (Metropolitan Sergii had claimed to have had 163 bishops in 1930) were dead, in exile in the forced-labor camps, in enforced retirement, or carrying on stealthily as clandestine clerics.

The church was at its lowest point. On any given day the state could have completed its long campaign against the church by closing the few remaining parishes and arresting the four remaining bishops. Nikolai's career, too, was probably at its lowest point, for arrest could come at any moment. Metropolitan Sergii, the *locum tenens*, had narrowly escaped arrest in 1937, and no bishop had any guarantee of immunity, regardless of how acceptable he made himself to the regime.

One of the most often repeated charges against the hierarchy of the Russian church during these years was that of collusion with the Secret Police in its campaign to destroy the church.[11] According to this charge, only those bishops remained free who served the Secret Police by informing on their fellow prelates. In effect, the worthy bishops were all arrested, and only those who were agents of the Secret Police remained at large.

There is no way either to verify or disprove these charges, of course. Especially during the periods of extreme tension, there is no doubt that the Secret Police would make use of any informant it could get, and certainly the regime could be expected to exercise some discrimination in its arrests, removing the most hostile clerics before those who had managed to make themselves less objectionable to the regime. To some extent, at least, a bishop's survival during these periods would seem to indicate that the regime, for one reason or another, considered that bishop less inimical to its desires than those whom it arrested.

But by the end of the purges this particular charge no longer made a great deal of sense. The attack on the episcopacy had by then progressed to such a point that not even the most supine willingness to submit to the state would guarantee immunity from arrest. If a bishop sternly refused to collaborate, he would certainly be arrested, but by the latter half of the thirties, even if a bishop surrendered completely to the state, he would just as certainly be arrested—with the exception of the four bishops who remained when the purges had ended.

III

War

IT WAS THE PARTITIONING of Poland in 1939 that brought a halt to the antireligious campaign. According to the secret protocol of the Molotov-Ribbentrop Agreement, the German government would not object to the Soviet Union's annexation of eastern areas of Poland if Germany should occupy the western areas. This agreement probably saved the Russian Orthodox Church from extinction. Similarly, Nikolai, for whose career a premature conclusion seemed imminent by the late thirties, could date his final rise to the peak of success from the partitioning of Poland.

When the Wehrmacht invaded Poland on September 1, 1939, and that invasion was not followed by any massive action by Poland's allies, Stalin found himself heir to the vast areas of the western Ukraine and Belorussia, and he very quickly extended his domination to the Baltic states as well.

In order to bring the predominantly religious population of these areas under control as quickly as possible, the services of the Russian Orthodox Church were needed. It was

felt that it could gain immediate hegemony over the Orthodox churches of the new domains and, because of the
similarity of its liturgical traditions, could facilitate the dissolution of the Eastern Rite, or Uniate, Catholic Church
organizations as well by forced conversion to Orthodoxy.

Thus for the first time since the Revolution the Soviet
regime felt that the Russian Orthodox Church might be able
to render it an important service, and so the regime immediately postponed any continuing action in its campaign to
eradicate the Russian Orthodox Church. What began in
1939 as a temporary truce was to develop within four years
into a complete abandonment of the drive to eradicate the
church. Instead, the state unwillingly accepted the church's
continued existence in order to profit from such services
as the church was able to render it. The earlier policy of
adamant hostility to the church gave way to a new policy
of negotiated concession, whereby the church, in return for
serving the needs of the state, won the minimal concessions
necessary to its continued existence. Thus the partitioning
of Poland opened a new page in the history of the church
in the USSR, a page that was not to be closed for two
decades.

Two of the remaining four bishops were transferred to
the newly acquired areas. Metropolitan Sergii (Voskresenskii), who was second only to the *locum tenens* in the hierarchy, was sent to Riga, where he became the patriarchal
exarch until he was condemned by the Moscow patriarchate
for his defection to the Germans when Russia entered the
war. Archbishop Nikolai was elevated to exarch of the
western Ukraine and Belorussia.

We know little or nothing concretely of Nikolai's activities during the two years that followed. His assignment was
to accomplish in the shortest possible time what had taken

the Soviet state with all its resources at least a decade to accomplish within Russia. To make the populations sub-servient to occupying powers—and to atheistic Communists at that—was no mean task and, if we may judge from the patterns within Russia during the twenties, required the closest possible cooperation between collaborating clerics and organs of state power. It was quite likely that the Soviet Secret Police was the chief punitive arm that would enforce Nikolai's work in the churches, and it seems all but impos-sible that he was able to avoid collaboration with the Secret Police during the course of his duties in his new domains.

Nikolai's name appears in the list of those who attended a church celebration in Moscow in 1940, and, according to his official biographer, he was promoted to the rank of metropolitan in March 1941. Almost immediately thereafter, a vast campaign of clandestine arrest and deportation of great masses of the population throughout the occupied area was carried out by the Soviet Secret Police. This campaign was highly organized and well coordinated, having been planned well in advance and mobilized by secret, detailed instructions, some of which were later captured by the Ger-mans. The agencies responsible for the arrest were instructed to select the most hostile elements of the local population for deportation. It is very likely that a good percentage of those most hostile to the occupying powers were also deeply involved in the religious life of the community. There is no evidence to suggest that Nikolai had any personal part in these deportations. It would be incredible, however, if they escaped his notice.

The deportation program was just being completed when its work was cut short by the German invasion on June 22, 1941. The invasion also put an end to Nikolai's work of bringing the churches under control. Whatever accomplishments Nikolai may have achieved during his brief tenure as exarch were immediately nullified by the rapid advance of the German armies.

The national emergency caused by the German invasion could scarcely have been a welcome omen for the Russian Orthodox Church. Always considered a decidedly unwelcome segment of the Soviet population, Christians had on countless occasions demonstrated their hostility to Soviet rule. If this had resulted in time of peace in arrests, imprisonments, and executions, how much more would the Soviet regime be tempted to remove this potentially disloyal element of the population summarily in time of war? To make matters worse, during the early weeks of the war millions of Soviet citizens, the majority of them religious, welcomed the Germans as liberators from the atheistic Soviet regime. This was especially true in the western Ukraine and Belorussia, and this fact could hardly make Nikolai's position more secure, inasmuch as he was accountable (deservedly or otherwise) for securing the loyalty of the religious population in these areas. Finally, Sergii, the exarch in Riga, had defected to the Germans. If its most trusted collaborator in the Russian Orthodox Church could betray it at the first opportunity, the Soviet state would be well justified in being equally suspicious of the loyalty of Nikolai.

Nikolai's position, however secure his collaboration with the interests of the Communist state may have made it, was extremely uncertain after the invasion of the Germans. The Soviet state was making a practice of shooting great numbers of politically undesirable elements—convicts and, in at least one instance, church members—in the face of the German advance, and that Nikolai as a leading representative of the distrusted church would escape such a fate was by no means certain.

As a matter of fact, Nikolai's attitude toward the German invasion remains unclear even in retrospect. There have been some reports that he was not even in the Ukraine at the time of the invasion. It is quite likely, however, that this version is misinformed, for according to *The Truth About Religion in Russia*, published in 1942 (which, incidentally, was the first book that the state had allowed the Russian Orthodox Church to publish since the Revolution), the German advance forced Nikolai to abandon his see at Lutsk. He spent the next three weeks close to the front exhorting the population to remain loyal to their Soviet motherland. Even though this book was edited by Nikolai himself, nothing is said about the circumstances of his evacuation of Lutsk—whether it was voluntary or by governmental order —nor is any information given of his precise whereabouts or the conditions in which he was active during the ensuing weeks. His actions, at least as reported later by the Russian Orthodox Church, appeared to be fully consonant with complete loyalty to the government. Whether these actions genuinely reflected his own sentiments, however, remains unclear. In the absence of further evidence there is at least room for the possibility that he may indeed have been awaiting an opportunity to defect.

On July 15 Metropolitan Sergii, the *locum tenens* in Moscow, appointed Nikolai Metropolitan of Kiev and Galicia, exarch of the entire Ukraine. According to Nikita Struve, a competent student of the Russian church, the appointment was probably motivated precisely by fear of Nikolai's eventual defection to the Germans. By appealing to his vanity, Sergii succeeded in inducing him to return to Moscow. Struve feels that the appointment was only an honorary gesture, for the German occupation of the Ukraine would make the appointment meaningless in any case.[1] By the end

of the third week of the war, however, German success in
the Ukraine may not have been so clearly predictable as it
is in retrospect, and it would seem just as likely that Nikolai's
transfer from the areas of the initial German advance to a
more westward area was a perfectly rational response by
the Moscow patriarchate to the rapidly developing situation.

More important is the fact that the mere elevation to
exarch of the Ukraine would, at the time, be a small inducement indeed. If Nikolai was considering defection his motivations would likely have been fear for his survival in the
wartime Soviet Union or, as in the case of Sergii of Riga, a
conviction that he could better aid the work of the church
from the German side of the line. In neither case would
a mere elevation in the hierarchy of a moribund church
offer more than the smallest inducement when compared
to the magnitude of the issues involved.

It is quite possible, however, that his feelings during this
period were not unmixed. While it is perfectly reasonable
to presume that the preceding decades of excesses by the
Soviet regime against his church and against his people
would lead Nikolai to welcome almost any alternative to
that regime, it is also possible that Nikolai's nationalistic
identification with his native land would prove stronger. As
the war progressed and the perils and sufferings of the Russian people multiplied, the threat to his people, his country,
his nation might have seemed more important than whatever
political disaffection he may have felt for the civil leadership
and its past policies.

Whatever his motivations, Nikolai did indeed return to
Moscow after receiving his new orders, reaching the capital
by August 3. The rapid deterioration of the war effort
made any thought of actually going to his new metropolitan

domains out of the question, and Nikolai remained in Moscow.

Throughout the summer of 1941 the German advance into Russia seemed invincible. Smolensk was under attack by mid-July. By the middle of September Kiev had fallen, and Leningrad was under siege. The German army in the Smolensk area, reinforced by the tanks earlier transferred to the Kiev campaign, resumed its advance on October 2. Two weeks later German armies were within sixty-three miles of Moscow.[2]

With the exception of the top levels of government, citizens of Moscow did not realize how critical the situation was in the first two weeks of October due to censorship of news. Earnest evacuation did not begin until October 5. It does not seem likely that church officials were well informed of the situation, and therefore it must have been somewhat of a surprise when, according to the account published some years later by the Moscow patriarchate, the executive committee of the local government ordered the evacuation of church officials on October 7.[3] For reasons that remain unclear, this order was not obeyed. In fact it is possible that such an order was not given at all on October 7, but the statement may have been a later invention designed to make the decision to evacuate the patriarchal party on October 14 seem less precipitate.

Doubtless, the government's decision to evacuate church officials rather than find some more drastic means of preventing their defection or capture came as a relief to the churchmen. It does not seem that the church knew of the decision in advance, for, in the address of the patriarchal *locum tenens* given that same day, there is no mention of any impending departure from Moscow, and indeed some parts of the message sound like an almost desperate attempt to convince the listeners of the patriotic loyalty of the church.

Nikolai was among those church officials who were evacuated. Later on a myth was promulgated that Nikolai had remained behind in Moscow when the patriarchate had evacuated so that he could continue to give spiritual leadership to the believers. It would appear that this myth enjoyed the official favor both of the church and of the government. In a book published in 1947 in tribute to the late Patriarch Sergii, Nikolai's evacuation is intentionally confused. While he is listed at one point as accompanying the evacuation party, in two other places in the book it is said that he remained in Moscow as Sergii's deputy. No editor, incidentally, is named for this collection, but probably Nikolai himself was the editor of this as of most other works published by the patriarchate in the wartime and early postwar periods.

The government also, it would seem, sought to enhance his record during this period, for it awarded him the medal "For the Defense of Moscow," conveniently overlooking the fact that Nikolai was nowhere in the vicinity during the Battle of Moscow. There is no evidence whatsoever that Nikolai was in Moscow at all during the period between the initial German advance on October 15 and the cessation of battle (because of winter) on December 8. Moscow was not again in immediate danger during the course of the war, and therefore Nikolai's reception of a medal for Moscow's defense seems somewhat incongruous and was probably designed to enhance Nikolai's reputation after the state had come to rely on his services.

Nevertheless, an award to Nikolai was not entirely misplaced, for he contributed enthusiastically to the war effort in the area of propaganda. And even though he was not per-

sonally involved in the defense of Moscow, he gave his
benediction to the efforts of those who had remained behind
when he evacuated:

In the days when the enemy hordes advanced on Moscow
and the enemy was already stretching his bloody hand toward
our capital, the Moscow pastors passionately called believers
from the church pulpits to sternness and manliness of spirit,
to unshakable faith that with the help of God we would preserve our capital from the enemy and his filthy boot would not
tread on our squares and streets; they blessed the inhabitants
for armed defense of the boundaries around Moscow and those
whose physical powers permitted participated themselves in
this holy work.

Fulfilling their duty to Country and capital, many of the
Moscow clergy in those days took part in the local organizations of air raid defense. Some of them even held commanding
posts in these organizations.[4]

With the USSR threatened, Nikolai felt nothing incompatible between the faith and active warfare. Like so many
other clergymen the world over, he felt the war a holy
cause for his side: "Not only sacred civil duty calls believers to the defense of Country, the duty of a believing
Christian also calls them to this: the teaching of Christ
requires of each of his followers whole-hearted love for his
Native Land and defense of it from the encroachments of
the enemy."[5]

Thus any possible ambiguity about support of the Soviet
government was overshadowed completely by the surge of
nationalism in Nikolai's wartime speeches. Nor did Nikolai
feel it necessary to remember any of the distasteful experiences he may have had during the preceding two years,
when he had been in the midst of the bitter hostility evoked
by the Soviet occupation in the annexed areas, or when, in

the first month of the war, he had been at the front and
surely must have witnessed the mood of the people of the
western Ukraine, millions of whom joyfully greeted the
German invaders as liberators. According to Nikolai:

Our Orthodox population in the Western provinces of the
Ukraine and Belorussia returned to the bosom of the mother
native land and Mother Church in September, 1939. From that
time it began to breathe deeply. For almost two years Orthodox people prayed freely in their Churches, and made enthusiastic pilgrimages to their holy monasteries. Parishes which
had been converted to Catholicism returned to Orthodoxy with
open manifestations of religious joy. These two years of the
life of the Western provinces of the Ukraine and Belorussia,
when they were united in the single family of the Soviet
peoples, were a happy, quiet epoch for the faithful.

It is not surprising that the news of Hitler's despicable attack
on our country aroused a wave of Christian patriotism in the
hearts of the Orthodox masses and inspired them to the defense
of their native land and the faith.[6]

Although the state had demonstrated a somewhat unexpected solicitude for the welfare of the church leaders by
evacuating them from Moscow to Ulyanovsk, several hundred miles to the east, it had as yet given little concrete in-
dication of the change in policy that within two years was
to revolutionize church-state relations in the Soviet Union.
The churchman whom the state selected for its first concrete
act in this direction was Nikolai. On November 2, 1941,
Nikolai was appointed to the Extraordinary State Commission of Inquiry on German crimes in occupied territory.[7]
This was a most significant appointment, for it marked the
first time that Stalin's government officially included a
churchman in any governmental body. (Nikolai appears to
have been in Ulyanovsk rather than Moscow at the time of

his appointment, for his signature is affixed to the patriarchal proclamation of November 24.[8] His signature is not absent from actions taken by the patriarchate at Ulyanovsk until January 1942, which would probably indicate that his return to Moscow came some time after his appointment to the Extraordinary State Commission.)

That Nikolai was able to be of effective service to the state is evident in the first publication of the Moscow patriarchate, edited by Nikolai in 1942, which contains a large section of letters, memoirs, and accounts of eyewitnesses to German atrocities against churches and church people.[9] This publication was primarily a work of wartime propaganda, meeting the needs of the state rather than those of the church, and ignoring the past quarter-century of similar lack of restraint by the Soviets. It is not unnatural for churchmen to be less critical of their government in time of national emergency, and in any case, Nikolai's position as a Christian did legitimately demand his outrage at bestial actions by the Germans. Therefore, whatever the ultimate use to which they were put, and regardless of the fact that they ignored similar outrages committed earlier by the Soviets, Nikolai's statements as a member of the Extraordinary State Commission were not necessarily incompatible with his vocation as a churchman.

The issue is not so clear, however, in the case of the Katyn Forest massacre. A mass grave containing some fourteen thousand bodies of Polish officers and intelligentsia had been discovered in eastern Poland, and the Germans gave wide publicity to the evidence that the massacres had taken place during the prewar Soviet occupation of the area. Consequently, when the Soviet armies returned, the Extraordinary Commission was dispatched to investigate. Nikolai took part in the investigation and wrote a long article,[10] which was later published in several languages, demonstrating that the massacre definitely was committed by the Germans, not the Soviets. From the total body of available evidence, however, it would seem all but conclusive that this atrocity was indeed committed by the Soviets themselves.[11]

Nikolai's vehement denial of such an opinion raises an interesting question of what his own reaction at the scene of the crime may have been. Considering the length of time that had elapsed since the perpetration of the act, it would seem difficult for an objective observer to be as absolutely convinced as Nikolai claimed to be that the Soviets could not possibly have been responsible. If the evidence did point to the Soviets as perpetrators of the crime, or if it even left room for doubt, such conflict in the evidence was not included in Nikolai's article.

It must remain a possibility, however, that Nikolai was unwitting of conflicting evidence. This would imply a rather strange degree of trust on Nikolai's part. He, after all, had personally witnessed many of the extremes of ruthlessness of which the Soviet state had shown itself capable during the preceding two decades—the church had been one of the chief recipients of state brutality—and, in addition, if he had the least acquaintance with Soviet antireligious propaganda he certainly must have been aware that the state was not above manipulating evidence to suit its purposes. Even if he were shown no conflicting evidence in the Katyn case, it would be difficult to understand his utter lack of skepticism concerning the evidence he was shown.

Nikolai received permission to return to Moscow more than a year before the *locum tenens* himself returned. At the beginning of 1942 he was in Moscow administering the affairs of the patriarchate. The dramatic lifting of the curfew on Easter eve, 1942, despite the danger of air raids, gives some insight into his position with the government at this time.[12] Nikolai certainly was not privy to the impending curfew relaxation prior to Easter eve, for the day before he issued an order to all clergy and believers in Moscow demanding strictest observations of curfew regulations.[13] The last-minute announcement that curfew would be suspended so that believers might celebrate Easter according to tradition may have come as a considerable surprise to Nikolai.

It seems most probable that this sudden decision in the Christians' favor was made by the state in order to avert the possibility of riot and strife in Moscow. It does not seem likely that the believers would have obeyed the curfew, for the Easter celebration enjoys such great popularity within Orthodoxy that it is certainly the most tenacious of all church festivities. The state may have realized that celebration of the festival in violation of the curfew could be averted only through massive use of force and most probably decided against risking turmoil in such a critical time of war. We do not know whether Nikolai was informed of this decision before it was announced in the evening papers, but it is certain he had no part in any discussions along these lines before the final hours.

Although Nikolai may not have gained the ear of the state by Easter, 1942, it seems quite evident that his position was becoming more and more secure in ensuing months. Beginning in mid-1942 the Russian Orthodox Church entered into collaboration with the state in preparing propaganda for distribution behind German lines.[14] The first recorded instance of church propaganda designed to encourage the resistance in the German rear came on June 22, 1942, when Nikolai prepared leaflets encouraging partisan activities for distribution in the occupied areas. Naturally, these leaflets were delivered by Soviet Army aircraft, which indicates that Nikolai was willing to lend the authority of his ecclesiastical position to the Soviet war effort, and that the government was willing to accept his service. On November 22 a joint letter appeared, signed by Nikolai and Metropolitan Sergii, seeking the support of Rumanian soldiers. The following month a similar appeal was made to the Rumanian church, this time by Sergii himself, and at Easter, 1943, Sergii similarly addressed himself to the Yugoslavs, Czechs, and Greeks.

Because the Soviet government apparently felt that these appeals were effective, the church became a participant in the pan-Slavic movement created by the Soviets to strengthen their war effort. Nikolai's talents as a propagandist made him an excellent choice for this activity, and his messages for the other Slavic peoples were fully as incendiary as was the rest of the wartime propaganda:

Our struggle with these enemies is the most holy duty of each Christian!

Dear Slavic Brothers! I want to tell you that our Orthodox Church, which in the course of all Russian history has lived one life with her people, now in the days of the Patriotic War, fully gives herself to the service of her Native Land and the Russian people in this year of difficult trials.

• • •

The Church is full of grief and holy hatred of the enemy. . . .
. . . We shall be united! In unity in battle shoulder to shoulder is our power! And God will help us in the holy work! Let an eternal stigma of infamy lie on those who now or later try to destroy Slavic unity!

• • •

The Russian Orthodox Church blesses you for the holy battle, dear brother Slavs![15]

On March 27, 1943, Nikolai participated in a second area of church collaboration with the Soviet war effort. As has been noted, large numbers of the Ukrainian population welcomed the German advance as liberation from the Soviet regime. Several schismatic Orthodox movements arose under the German occupation, which no longer accepted the ecclesiastical jurisdiction of the Muscovite church. The most notable of these movements was the Ukrainian Autocephalous Church led by Archbishop Polycarp. During the twenties, when the Living Church Adventure was contributing greatly to jurisdictional confusion in the Ukraine, Polycarp had been involved in an earlier attempt to gain independence from the Moscow church. Even at that time it seemed apparent that the Ukrainian church movement was inspired as much by nationalistic aspirations of the Ukrainian people as by ecclesiastical reasons. Certainly during World War II Polycarp's movement became a focus for Ukrainian nationalism.

Thus the movement represented an ecclesiastical schism to the Russian Orthodox Church and at the same time seemed a political challenge to the Soviet state. This issue was an ideal demonstration of an area in which the desires of the church coincided with those of the state. The council of bishops that condemned Polycarp in 1943 served both an ecclesiastical and a political end. Nikolai, of course, participated in the council and thus was able to give practical demonstration of one area at least in which church and state could collaborate to mutual advantage.

A third way in which the church contributed to the war effort was through its ability to mobilize the monetary donations of believers. Millions of rubles were collected by the church for the state's military needs. Nikolai apparently found such activity congenial to his own attitudes during the war, as witness his dedication of a column of tanks:

And she [the church] now is proud that our column of tanks named for Dmitrii Donskoi, armed by Church-wide donations, undertakes its duty in the holy business of the destruction of

the hordes of German bandits. In my person she is fortunate to
see with her own eyes these dread tanks built from the means
of believers and clergy of our country, and you, to whom has
fallen the honored lot of taking these tanks into battle.

In the name of Patriarch Sergii, in my name, in the name of
all our Church, I wish to tell you, dear brother soldiers, from
the depths of my heart: God will help you in your holy business of defense of Country! Let these war machines, led to
victory by our will, stern as granite, bring vengeance and death
to the fascist butchers of our people, who have tormented and
flooded with blood a part of our holy Country. These satanists
—enemies of our culture and the people's happiness, enemies
of mankind unworthy to bear the name of human, unworthy
to live on the earth! ...

Forward, dear soldiers, in the name of the full cleansing of
our country from fascist filth, in the name of peaceful life and
happiness of the people! To the holy business—forward![16]

The dramatic change in Soviet policy toward religion,
which came with the concordat of September 1943, was not
gratuitous, for the church had already demonstrated that
its continued existence in the Soviet Union could be of considerable benefit to the state. The magnitude of the change
in state policy in September, however, would suggest that
considerable negotiations preceded the formal announcement of the new course. It is quite likely that Nikolai bore
the major burden of the initial stages of the negotiations.
Sergii, the *locum tenens*, did not return to Moscow until
August 1943, and Nikolai's growing access to governmental
leaders may have effected his return from Ulyanovsk.

By early September the agreement apparently had reached
a mutually satisfactory form. On September 4, 1943, Nikolai,
Aleksii, and Sergii met with Stalin in private audience. The
story was carried in *Izvestiia* the next morning.[17] This was
the first time since the Revolution that the leadership of the
church had been in direct, publicized conversation with the

head of the Soviet state. It marked the beginning of what was to be a new relationship between church and state in the USSR, a relationship that would remain in force relatively unchanged for the rest of Nikolai's life.

The new relationship, which had doubtless been negotiated over the preceding months and was formally accepted in the interview with Stalin, amounted to an unwritten concordat between church and state. For the church's part the new relationship consisted of full political collaboration with the Soviet state in all areas wherein such collaboration might be effective. This was not a new position for the church. It had been the church's approach to political matters since 1927, and for a great part of Nikolai's life had doubtless been his own political position. The difference was that now the state was publicly accepting that support and in return was granting certain limited concessions necessary to the life of the church. This would remain the pattern for the next two decades, and Nikolai would be the point at which church and state policy met.

At the time, the church was serving the political needs of the state by strengthening the morale of the people, by urging resistance and censuring collaboration behind German lines both in Russia and in eastern Europe, and by collecting money for the war effort. As the subsequent months were to demonstrate, it would also contribute to Soviet agitation for a second front on the part of the Americans and British, and would lend its support to the state's propaganda campaign against the Roman Catholic Church. For its part, the state was prepared to give concessions to the church, consisting of legal recognition of the church (including permission to elect a patriarch), permission for training of priests, printing of literature, reopening of a limited number of churches, and religious instruction of children. All of these had been denied to the church during the preceding decade, and ever since the Soviet accession to power the church's ability to act in all of these areas had been under great pressure.

Three days later a council was convened to elect a patriarch. The agreement had certainly been reached long before the interview with Stalin, for considerable time must have been required to organize the council. Three days would have been little enough time to allow for the travel of bishops from outlying areas even in peacetime, and considering the wartime burdens on the transportation system, the planning for the council must have taken place a great deal earlier. There have been rumors that the Secret Police hurriedly searched the prisons and forced-labor camps in order to find bishops who could attend the council and bolster its pitifully slim attendance. Whether this be true or not, only nineteen bishops attended the council. It must have been painfully evident to those present how many of their numbers were still in exile and how many more had disappeared without trace. The nineteen participants stood in bleak contrast to the hundreds of delegates to the council of 1917, which preceded this one, and even though the deplorable conditions in which the church found itself after a quarter-century of Soviet rule must have been paramount in the minds of those present, no reflection of that factor appeared in the speeches. The propaganda messages delivered by the council, in which Nikolai played no small role, were full of loyalty and gratitude to the Soviet government and were without a hint of that ambivalence which the decimated ranks of the bishops might have elicited.

The council apparently was convened only to accomplish two purposes. The first, of course, was to elect Sergii patriarch. He had been the patriarchal *locum tenens* for seventeen years and had been identified with what was now to be the accepted political position of the church. This was done

on Aleksii's motion, which may imply that Aleksii already
was being groomed to replace the aged Sergii. The other
function of the council was to give full ecclesiastical condemnation to those bishops who had defected to the Germans.[18]

True to its bargain, the state quickly established the Council for the Affairs of the Russian Orthodox Church under
the governmental Council of Ministers. At the head of this
council was Georgii G. Karpov, a high officer in the Secret
Police. A network of regional, provincial, and local offices
of this council very quickly came into existence, so quickly
in fact that it seems likely that these were not new creations
but merely an administrative redesignation of a network for
control of the churches previously existing within the
NKVD. In any case, it seems unlikely that the Secret Police
remained ignorant of the new arrangements, and this agency
of state power was to remain a permanent factor in Nikolai's
life.[19]

Even though Aleksii played a prominent role at the council of 1942, Nikolai seems to have been given the chief
responsibilities in the newly reorganized church. He was
placed in charge of church publications, which, in view of
the controlled press in the Soviet Union, was a highly sensitive position. More important for Nikolai's life, he was to
be entrusted with directing the foreign affairs of the Russian
Orthodox Church. It would appear that in the months immediately following the council he devoted considerable
attention to this area as the church sought to continue its
work with populations under German control.

As the tide of battle reversed and the Red Army began its
advance to the west, the room for such activity continued
to expand. Nikolai retained his designation as metropolitan
of Kiev and Galicia, and as the German armies began to be
rolled back out of the Ukraine, Nikolai inherited the chief

responsibility for reasserting ecclesiastical control over the religious population of the newly liberated areas. Reprisals were carried out by the state against those who had collaborated with the Germans,[20] and inasmuch as many religious Ukrainians had welcomed the Germans, Nikolai must have been privy to some of these reprisals. Regardless of how distasteful he may have found such vengeance, he was scarcely in a position to diminish greatly the ferocity of the reprisals or to protest against them.

The death of Patriarch Sergii on May 15, 1944, was not unexpected, for Sergii's health had been poor for several years. The death of the patriarch necessitated a new council to elect a successor. That nearly a year elapsed before the council was convened probably indicates that this council was intended to accomplish a great deal more than had the council of 1943.

The council of 1945 drew up a set of rules for the inner structure of the church. It would be unwise to think that the state was uninterested in these rules; in actual fact the new statutes of the church probably had to be agreed upon in advance in point-by-point negotiation with the government. It is not known how or when these negotiations were conducted. We are told that Nikolai was Aleksii's assistant in planning the council. It is just as likely to have been the other way around.[21]

One of the novel features of the council, which convened on January 31, 1945, was that it was attended by representatives of major national churches throughout the Orthodox world. When the council met, among those present in Moscow were the patriarchs of Alexandria and Antioch; the catholicos of the Georgian church; and representatives of the Ecumenical Patriarch, the Patriarch of Jerusalem, and the Serbian and Rumanian churches. In addition, Metropolitan Veniamin, exarch of the Moscow patriarchate in North and South America, was present, as were a number of non-Orthodox Western dignitaries (following the precedent set by the Archbishop of Canterbury, who had attended the council of 1943). It was Nikolai who gave the speeches of greeting to these honored guests.

The visits of such dignitaries obviously required advance planning, planning for which Nikolai was responsible. Apparently the Moscow patriarchate was already considering the course its policy would take during the next three years. It was about to begin a campaign to gain hegemony over the Orthodox world. Nikolai, working in collaboration with the state, was the architect of this campaign.

The formal purpose of the council was accomplished in short order. Aleksii had been the appointed successor to Sergii when the latter's will had been "discovered" at his death. Quite predictably, Aleksii was unanimously elected the next patriarch.[22]

It seems somewhat incongruous that Aleksii succeeded Patriarch Sergii.[23] Nikolai at this time was by far the more prominent, both in terms of public recognition and, much more importantly, in usefulness to the Soviet state. It may be that Aleksii was named patriarch against the wishes of the state as the church, true to the desires of its decedant patriarch, independently expressed its own will in the matter. This does not seem likely. It is far more probable that the state considered the position of titular head of the church much less important operationally, and preferred to have this position go to Aleksii, who was senior to Nikolai both in age and in ordination, while retaining its favorite, Nikolai, in an apparently inferior position. The state quite obviously had grand designs for Nikolai in the coming years.

IV

Empire[1]

THE COUNCIL OF 1945 was extraordinarily successful. A new patriarch, Aleksii, had been elected without incident, and guidelines for the administration of the church had been established. More important to the Soviet state, however, were two additional benefits achieved at the council. Dignitaries from throughout the Orthodox world had shown by their willingness to attend the council the great potential influence that the patriarch of the Russian Orthodox Church continued to wield in areas outside the confines of the USSR. Several of these foreign delegates had also participated to some degree in the production of speeches, statements, and messages that could be directly applicable to the aims of Soviet propaganda. Thus the council of 1945 gave ample vindication to the fact that had gradually become apparent during the preceding years: collaboration with the Russian Orthodox Church could be of definite value to the interests of the Soviet state, especially in its relations with its neighbors.

The government does not appear to have been fully convinced of the fruitfulness of cooperating with the church in foreign affairs prior to the successful proceedings of this council. It is true that the government had allowed whatever permits were necessary for the foreign visitors' participation, and in addition had supplied aircraft for their transportation. But the state does not appear to have shown a great deal of interest in the proceedings, and the subsequent development of the collaboration of the Russian Orthodox Church in Soviet foreign policy would seem to indicate that the state was not truly convinced of the validity of such cooperation until the successful conclusion of the 1945 council.

Thus it would appear unlikely that the Soviet government had taken a leading part in securing the participation of foreign churchmen in the 1945 council. And if initiative for this move was supplied by the regime, then it would seem probable that this maneuver was undertaken as an experiment, and no great conviction of its usefulness lay behind the initiative.

It is much more likely that the invitation of foreign observers was an idea originally conceived by the church. In fact, it is not improbable that Nikolai himself, because of his recent experience in dealing with other Orthodox, conceived of the idea. If the church did indeed originate the plan, then apparently Nikolai and Aleksii were able to convince the Soviet government of its potential usefulness, at least to the extent of gaining governmental permission to try an experiment in this direction.

It was a successful experiment. The council of 1945 served as a practical demonstration both of the general direction church collaboration with Soviet foreign policy was to take in the future and, more specifically, as the model of a major campaign by the Russian Orthodox Church to gain predominance over the entire Orthodox East within the next three years.[2]

The new policy in the Soviet use of religion in foreign affairs was not formally ratified at the council itself, but shortly thereafter. Stalin had returned from the Yalta Conference at the end of February, and on April 10, he and Molotov received Aleksii, Nikolai, and the priest Kolchitskii in private audience. Stalin's first personal meeting with churchmen in 1943 had introduced the new policy on religion within the Soviet Union. This second (and last) meeting served similarly to initiate the new policy in foreign affairs.

A grand vista of expansion lay before Stalin as a result of the Yalta Conference. The Red Army's advance was sweeping over what enemy resistance remained, and the Yalta agreements indicated that Stalin would have the opportunity of gaining permanent control in areas liberated by the Red Army. All of eastern Europe lay within his reach. In western Europe the commanding role played by the Communist parties of Italy and France in the liberation of those countries seemed to suggest that Communist control of western Europe might be possible in a very short time. England, because of Churchill's antipathy toward communism, remained a problem, but there was every hope of neutralizing England's hostility by building upon the warm afterglow of the wartime alliance. The United States posed no immediate threat because of Roosevelt's ready acceptance of the image of Stalin as a leader who had abandoned communism for Russian nationalism. The secret protocol of the Yalta Conference, whereby the USSR would enter the war against Japan immediately after the defeat of Germany, seemed to assure the extension of Soviet influence in the Far East. This, together with the wartime rise of Mao Tse-tung's strength in China, seemed to assure the Soviet Union of eventual hegemony in that part of the world.[3]

To be sure, there were difficulties for Stalin to face. The USSR was scarcely in a position to undertake new expansion in 1945. The military was strong, but the economy was much overextended, the people were exhausted, and the resources of the country were strained to the limit. Time— several years at least—would be required for the country to rebuild. In addition, even in 1945 the beginning of the cold war could be discerned on the horizon. Thus Stalin could scarcely afford to be too sanguine in his hopes for conquest.

Nevertheless he retained a strongly expansionistic bent, and, despite the need for reconstruction at home, he was fully prepared to attempt such expansion as was possible, especially if conquest could be won by nonmilitary or paramilitary means.

The church's role in the plan of conquest was apparently a major topic of discussion on April 10. The council of 1945 had demonstrated the ability of the church to influence the Orthodox leadership of eastern Europe and the Near East. The task of the church was now to capitalize upon this ability. Its assignment was twofold. First, it was to attempt to bring all the other Orthodox churches under Russian Orthodox ecclesiastical domination. Thus the Soviet state, through the Russian church, would secure control. This was its primary task. Its second and far less important task was to use its influence in Orthodox countries to generate responses that could contribute to the propaganda campaign that would accompany the expansion of Soviet influence. Because of the size of the Orthodox population in these areas, the contribution that the church could make to Soviet foreign policy would be enormous.

The church was to pursue the same two objectives in

western Europe. Because the Communist rise to power was
not so imminent, and especially because of the relatively
small size of the Orthodox population of western Europe, the
immediate contribution of the church would naturally be
less significant in these areas. Nevertheless, if the Moscow
patriarchate could successfully bring the Orthodox communities in western Europe under its jurisdictional control, this
would serve admirably as an auxiliary base of operations in
the attempt by the rather large Communist parties in these
areas to achieve political power.

England did not possess a sizable Orthodox minority,
and thus Stalin could scarcely hope to establish a base of
eventual political power through the church there. However, the services of the Russian Orthodox Church in Soviet
relations with Great Britain were important for Stalin's
plans for expansion. From the time of the Revolution until
the crisis of World War II, the Church of England had
been one of the major voices in the campaign of protest
against Soviet religious policy. If British hostility to the imminent expansion of Soviet control were to be averted it was
essential that this voice of protest remain silent. It was the
task of the Russian Orthodox Church to secure this silence.
At the time it would probably have appeared that this assignment was the most difficult and the one least likely to
succeed. The Church of England, however, had a long history of interest in Russian Orthodoxy and had even sent
its primate on a visit to the Soviet Union in 1943. If the
Russian Orthodox Church could build on this historic interest, it seemed at least possible that the hostility of the
preceding quarter-century could be undone.

The United States appeared to occupy a much lower position in the priority of church collaboration with Soviet
foreign policy. The United States was far away, and, be-

cause of its acceptance of the friendship of the wartime alliance, seemed unlikely to interfere with Soviet plans for expansion in the immediate future. Nevertheless, since the United States maintained a sizable Russian Orthodox community, the church not only would be able to provide good propaganda for the Soviet state, but would also serve as an aid to the American Communist Party.

The church had a relatively minuscule field of activity in the Far East, and hence its services there would be completely peripheral. It could hope to gain control over the sizable Orthodox community at Harbin in Manchuria, however.

This then was the basic outline of Russian Orthodoxy's— and Nikolai's—role in the Soviet plan of expansion. He took part in the formal ratification of this plan with Stalin on April 10, 1945. More and more, the activity of the church in Soviet foreign affairs would be identified almost exclusively with Nikolai as the head of the church's Department of External Relations. Intimately involved in the questions of church-state relations, Nikolai was certainly confronted with the ethical dimensions of such collaboration with the Soviet regime.

The basic question of collaboration between church and state would not in itself raise any particular problems of conscience for Russian Orthodoxy. Separation of church and state was by no means an ideal of the church.[4] Quite the contrary, separation of church and state was an ideal identified with communism in the Soviet Union. The first legal expression of this ideal had been made by the Communists themselves in January 1918, and was met immediately by a violent denunciation on the part of the Orthodox Church. Separation of church and state was identified with the Communist regime in the minds of churchmen. That the new foreign policy contemplated by the church in 1943 would trespass against that ideal could scarcely have caused Nikolai grave problems of conscience.

The Russian Orthodox Church had a long tradition of close collaboration with the state. Indeed, the subservience of the church to the state had been a theological virtue in prerevolutionary Orthodoxy. According to the ecclesiology of that period, the head of the church on earth was the Orthodox tsar, and it was precisely in subjection to his rule that the nature of the church resided. State and church were merely two inseparable aspects of God's ordained order, and the church therefore was duty bound to its ruler the tsar.

So important was this identification of church and state to Orthodoxy that a considerable number of Orthodox churchmen were unable to conceive of the continued existence of the church after the fall of the monarchy. Some high churchmen felt their first duty after the February Revolution was to work for the restitution of the monarchy, lest Orthodoxy cease to exist. And even under the Provisional Government of 1917, the church had at no time sought to be free of state support, but sought to work out a new form of church-state cooperation under which the head of state would be required to be of the Orthodox faith and thus able to be at the same time the head of the church.

Therefore, there was ample historical and traditional justification for the collaboration of the church with the civil authority. In 1945, however, the church yielded (at least in foreign affairs) to an atheistic state, one of whose proclaimed objectives was the ultimate disappearance of all religion from the earth. Surely, then, the older theology, in which the head of church and head of state were united in one person, could scarcely apply under the changed conditions.

Great numbers of churchmen had abandoned the legalized

Russian Orthodox Church precisely over the issue of co-existence with an atheist state. To the extent that underground Orthodoxy in the USSR had any ideological or theological platform, it was precisely this issue that was at the center. The degree of strength reached by this underground movement prior to its disruption by the police in the early thirties and the revival of underground Orthodoxy during the war could scarcely have permitted one such as Nikolai to remain ignorant of this point of view.[5]

There was a more immediate ethical question involved, however. Russian Orthodoxy had long and bitter experience of what Communist rule means to the life of the church. The church had very nearly been destroyed before World War II. If its own experience was to be any criterion, Communist accession to power elsewhere would almost certainly be followed by the diminishing and perhaps the eventual demise of the work of the churches in the areas involved. As a churchman Nikolai was committed to Christianity. Yet in the meeting with Stalin in 1945 he took a position that could not but contribute to the expansion of communism and the corresponding diminution of the work of Christianity. Therefore his agreement to collaborate with Soviet foreign policy implied a necessary conflict with his commitment as a churchman.

Furthermore, this collaboration would certainly mean suffering and death for individual Christians. Legions of Orthodox people whose only crime was their belief were in 1945 serving terms in the forced-labor camps, and millions had lost their lives for their faith. To cooperate with Soviet policies of foreign expansion could only mean that Russian Orthodoxy's tragic story might be repeated in each of the new domains. Thus even in 1945 there was an obvious possibility that Nikolai's work might cause suffering and death to innocent people.

There is the question, however, of Stalin's changed public image during the war years. Many in the West felt that the long-awaited transformation had finally come, that Stalin, who from his first speech after the invasion had discarded the role of leader of international communism for that of a Russian patriot, had undergone a profound change, and that the dark sides of Communist rule in Russia were finally a thing of the past.[6] This was widely believed in the West; if it was similarly believed within the USSR, that would only suggest a perfectly astonishing degree of credulity among the Russian people. Especially for one such as Nikolai, who had had long and intimate experience with the realities of Communist rule in Russia, such credulity would be quite out of the question. In view of such experience, even the most optimistic of men would require far more convincing evidence of a basic change in the nature of the regime than had appeared by 1945.

The most obvious rationale for explaining a churchman's collaboration with state activity that may be against the interests of the churches and people of a foreign country is to be found in his nationalistic sentiments. It would not be unnatural for a churchman to feel that because he is himself a Russian and has been entrusted with a responsibility for the Russian Orthodox Church, his chief and only duty is to his own church. It is entirely likely that such collaboration with the foreign policy of the Soviet state was absolutely necessary to the continued existence of the church within Russia. If the church were to survive in the USSR, it must find some way to diminish the hostile activity of the state, and collaboration with Soviet foreign policy apparently was the price demanded for its continued existence within Russia. Thus a churchman who found himself in Nikolai's position could possibly dismiss the question of the effects of his actions on foreign Christians by appealing in his own mind to his first duty to the church in Russia.

A more subtle rationale is to be found in the doctrine of the lesser evil. Perhaps one could feel that the expansion of communism was inevitable. Whether or not Russian Orthodoxy aided it, the Soviet state would gain domination over eastern Europe and elsewhere. Since Christians in those areas would have to live under communism in any case, perhaps one such as Nikolai was uniquely able to serve in some small way to ameliorate their harsh lot. Certainly the Russian Orthodox Church had the most experience in living under communism and it had learned what was possible and what was not. Certainly it knew that the normal first reaction of violent hostility would bring to the Christian and to his church only hardship, suffering, and death. The Russian church, by gaining dominance over the churches in the newly acquired areas, could at least save them the bitter experience of experimentation and by guiding their policy could show them the way of least hardship. If Communist rule were inevitable, then surely the Russian Orthodox Church with Nikolai as its spokesman was best qualified by experience to lead the churches in the hostile new environment.

In addition, one could make a positive case for such collaboration. While there is no denying the dark side of Communist rule, perhaps a Christian might find in the communist ideals of social justice, many of them derived from Christianity, sufficient incentive to justify such collaboration. Communist theory, especially in its humanism, can be highly attractive, particularly when compared with existing social

conditions in areas that have had little contact with en-
lightened government.[7]

But these explanations can hardly be satisfactory in the
last analysis. A Russian churchman could hardly remain
blind to the vast gulf that exists between the humanistic
ideals of communist theory and the bitter realities of its
practice during the preceding decades. There is a difference
between showing other churches the way of least suffering
and becoming a part of that which would deny them the
possibility of seeking alternative ways. And surely one's
duty to his own church cannot free him from responsibility
for other churches, other Christians, as well as his own.

The new policy was put into effect almost immediately.
The Orthodox churches of eastern Europe were brought
under Moscovite domination within the three months immediately following the audience with Stalin. Perhaps because of the presence of the Red Army, the actual negotiations with these churches did not require Nikolai's presence
but were accomplished by subordinates. Chief among Nikolai's subordinates appeared to be Archbishop Grigorii, who
very quickly restored a desirable order to the Estonian
Orthodox Church, then went to Bulgaria to secure their
acceptance of Russian Orthodox leadership. Grigorii may
have been able to use the Bulgarian church's fear of Roman
Catholicism in persuading them to accept Moscow's domination. Rumania apparently did not require a special delegation but affiliated with the Russian church almost immediately. The Serbian (Yugoslav) church was brought into the
family in April.

The plan was proceeding well among the Orthodox
churches of eastern Europe, and the next step of the operation was activated very quickly. This second phase involved
attempting to gain Russian Orthodox hegemony over the

Orthodox churches outside the areas immediately threatened by Soviet occupation. On May 28 Patriarch Aleksii, Nikolai, and a considerable retinue departed for a trip through the Middle East. Their first week was in the Holy Land. This, of course, was a well-conceived itinerary, for this visit was the first time in history that a Russian Orthodox patriarch had visited Jerusalem. Hence the occasion served to ensure maximum publicity for the ecclesiastical delegation. A Soviet plane was provided by the government, with a "Hero of the Soviet Union" as its pilot, a factor that also would not be ignored by the press.

On the way to Jerusalem the party had stopped to meet with representatives of the Armenian church, and had been joined in Damascus by Alexander, patriarch of Antioch. Patriarch Alexander accompanied the Russian party for the remainder of the tour of the Middle East. Subsequently it became known that the friendship of the Antioch church to Russia was not gratuitous but, on the contrary, was achieved through cash subsidies coming directly or indirectly from the Soviet government.

The Russian visitors conducted themselves most circumspectly during their sojourn in Palestine, spending their time meeting with the patriarch of the Jerusalem church and his staff and visiting various shrines of the Christian faith. Not a word was spoken about political matters. To all intents and purposes, the visitors from the Russian church were completely unconcerned with matters political and were present only in search of friendly relations with their sister church in Jerusalem. The party from Moscow did meet considerable opposition at the Russian Orthodox Church in Jerusalem, which was under the jurisdiction of the Synod Abroad, the most vehemently anti-Communist of the *émigré* Russian jurisdictions. However, the patriarch and his party were able to take this hostility in stride without loss of composure.

On June 5 the party proceeded on to Egypt, meeting with Patriarch Christopher the following day. On June 11 the three patriarchs were received by King Farouk. Nikolai's role in the Middle Eastern journey had already been completed, however, for on June 10 he and two others had departed for London.

Even the brief fortnight that Nikolai had already spent with the patriarchal party had demonstrated that the foreign activities of Russian Orthodox churchmen were to be under the close supervision of the worldwide intelligence apparatus of the Soviet Secret Police. It appears that the first concern of the church delegation upon arrival in a foreign city was to confer immediately with the local Soviet consul or embassy. It was the Soviet consulates and embassies, of course, that served as the area headquarters for the Soviet intelligence network.[8] Hence it is quite probable that one of the purposes of the first visit was to coordinate their intended activities with the local apparatus of Soviet intelligence and to receive whatever instructions the clandestine arm of Soviet foreign policy might have for them.

In addition to being under the immediate supervision of local Soviet intelligence officers, the patriarchal party was also under day-to-day supervision of representatives of the Soviet Secret Police traveling within the delegation.[9] Naturally, there is no concrete information as to which members of the patriarchal party were serving as the agents of Soviet control over the group. While every member of the delegation had doubtless been thoroughly checked by the Soviet state prior to receiving permission to join the tour, it was always the practice of the Soviet state to include direct officers of the Secret Police in disguise in the party, or at the very least to have among the members one or more trusted agents to ensure continued state surveillance. It is possible that Nikolai was fulfilling this role[10]; however, it would appear more likely that Nikolai had not at this time achieved the complete confidence of the state, but direct control was exercised through other agents in the party.

In this regard it is interesting that one of the members of the party was Vitalii, Archbishop of Tul's and Belev. Vitalii had been a member of the Living Church schism and had not repented of this action against the mother church until after the rapprochement of 1943. Inasmuch as the Living Church was vigorously encouraged by the Soviet state, he had doubtless entered into a relationship of close collaboration with the Soviet Secret Police in the twenties, and hence had had twenty years of close relation with representatives of the regime. It would seem odd indeed that an archbishop so recently received again into the body of the church, and who had had such an irregular history, would have been included in the patriarchal party, unless, of course, the state had suggested that he accompany the other churchmen.[11]

Thus, Church activity outside of Russia required intimate contact with the Soviet Secret Police. This was a factor Nikolai would have to live with throughout his service as head of the foreign affairs of Russian Orthodoxy. The state would not be satisfied merely with liaison but would require personal cooperation with the Soviet Secret Service outside the country.

A dramatic illustration of this aspect of Nikolai's ecclesiastical service was given in 1959 by Petr S. Deriabin. Deriabin was a high officer of the MVD who defected to the West and who, in his service in the Soviet Foreign Intelligence apparatus in Vienna, came into contact with Metropolitan Nikolai in 1953. According to Deriabin:

The telegram [from Moscow] said that Metropolitan Nikolai is an agent of State Security. The telegram stated that he is a high ranking Archbishop in the Orthodox Church and try not to make open to other people that he is the agent of the State Security and to use this material only if necessary and be very circumspect about the whole thing.

. . . Gus'kow [in charge of religious activities of the Soviet Intelligence apparatus of Vienna] told me that Metropolitan Nikolai and he were "brothers." Well, this is language—I mean both of them—they are State Security agents.[12]

He [Nikolai] is not a member of KGB, but he is an agent of KGB since World War II, who gives information to KGB. KGB is asking him and he is giving information. He is actually an agent.[13]

Deriabin describes in detail a mission that Nikolai performed at that time for the MVD. An Orthodox priest in Vienna had been recruited by the MVD through use of blackmail, and it was feared that he was planning to escape to Switzerland. Nikolai was assigned the task (which he successfully carried out) of ensuring that the priest would not try to escape. At the conclusion of this assignment, Nikolai mentioned that he felt that the matter had been mishandled by the local MVD and suggested that the priest's cooperation could probably be better secured by assigning to him a different local MVD contact than his present one.

It seems amply clear, then, that Nikolai's cooperation with the state involved intimate contact with the MVD. This could not avoid raising a dilemma. It is impossible that Nikolai could have retained any illusions about the character of the Soviet Secret Police. He himself had been imprisoned by the Secret Police and had been a witness to the vast destruction that its agents had wreaked on the church prior to World War II. The brutality and immorality of Secret Police agents was notorious throughout the Soviet Union, and Nikolai could scarcely have been ignorant that his collaboration with the MVD would involve his serving an element of Communist rule for whom any degree of morality had no claim whatsoever. To receive instructions from such an element inevitably and immediately would raise a question of conscience.

In addition, at least in this one known case the requirements of the MVD necessitated his acting against the interests of one of his coreligionists. In his contact with the priest in Vienna he became a direct party to blackmail and used the power of his ecclesiastical position to persuade the person to give up freedom for servitude to irreligious masters. It is one thing to serve the Soviet state when there is no alternative; but the priest in Vienna at least had an alternative, and Nikolai was instrumental in his losing it.

In Nikolai's favor, it is true that he attempted to secure for this priest a more congenial contact man with the MVD. According to Deriabin, Nikolai's only interest was greater efficiency in the intelligence operation. It is possible, however, that Nikolai was doing what little he could to ameliorate the difficult position the priest was in. Perhaps he reasoned that he had no alternative but to collaborate with the MVD in this matter, and intelligently sought what may have been the only possible way of acting, at least to some small degree, in the priest's interests as well.

This, then, was another of the dilemmas that Nikolai inherited with his rise to prominence in Russian Orthodoxy. It was a dilemma probably clear to him from the start, but certainly abundantly demonstrated on his first mission abroad in 1945. Even after he left the traveling party at Cairo, he could not feel himself free of the Secret Police, for he could not be certain that one or both of his companions to London were not serving to keep him under surveillance by the Soviet police.

Nikolai's visit to London was a resounding success. After first checking in with the Soviet Embassy there, he conferred with the Archbishop of Canterbury, with the Assembly of Bishops of the Anglican Church, with leaders of Parliament, with a leading rabbi in London, and held a press conference immediately before a personal audience with the King of England. Nikolai's talents for such work were immediately apparent: he could be most charming, urbane, sophisticated, and intelligent, and this was never more evident than in his first venture in foreign affairs. The English church was thoroughly charmed by him, and the animosities of preceding decades were immediately forgotten as the church gave voice to its historical support and friendship for the Russian Orthodox Church. If Nikolai's task was to prevent a resumption of prewar ecclesiastical hostility to Soviet religious policy, then his few days in London were eminently successful and seemed to promise that the churches in England would not interfere with the Soviet plan of expansion.

Nikolai did not enjoy immediate success in bringing the small colony of Russian Orthodox in London under Muscovite jurisdiction. But because of the relative weakness of Orthodoxy in England, this was a minor consideration, and was probably lost sight of entirely in view of the excellent results of his work with the English church. Nikolai also attempted to persuade Russian émigrés in London to return to the homeland, but we are not told whether he had any notable success.

The visit to England, apparently, was partly experimental. Nikolai had gone to one of the areas least critical for Soviet plans of expansion, and that seemed to offer little chance for success. He nevertheless had been able to demonstrate the results that this sort of work in the West could achieve. His return to Moscow was in triumph, but the most critical area, western Europe, still lay ahead.

The Russian Orthodox emigration in Europe was divided into two major groups. A large number of parishes in France were under the leadership of Metropolitan Evlogii, who had entered into the jurisdiction of the Ecumenical Patriarch in Constantinople after his condemnation by Moscow in the thirties. The more canonically prestigious and, at least before the war, the more numerous jurisdiction was that of the Synod Abroad. Unlike Evlogii, whose interests were comparatively nonpolitical, the Synod Abroad was violently anti-Communist and contained the most vehement enemies of Communist rule in Russia, many of whom had fought against bolshevism during the Civil War in Russia.

World War II, however, had brought disaster to the synod orientation, for in its single-minded obsession with the evil of communism, they had enthusiastically supported Hitler's invasion of Russia as an almost religious crusade against communism. Naturally, the defeat of Germany and the strong revulsion against the Nazi atrocities, which came to light during and immediately after the war, destroyed all of the Synod's prestige. It still contained a large number of high Russian Orthodox prelates and hence was able to rival the Moscow church leaders, but its moral authority was at a low ebb immediately after the war. Thus, in areas of Soviet occupation the Synod was not a problem for Soviet foreign policy. Because they were compromised by support of the Nazis, such churchmen could not possibly be an impediment to Soviet suzerainty in those areas. The MVD could coerce their cooperation by threat of punishment for war crimes, or, if they refused, could eliminate them by carrying out that threat.

Because some of the Synod parishes were in the West, however, they did remain a problem (albeit a relatively minor one) for the church's consideration. Hence, on August 10, 1945, the Moscow patriarchate, which had already condemned the Synod a dozen years earlier, addressed the following note to its leaders:

Having tried absolutely all means for preserving the peace and unity of the Church and for the conversion of those who have renounced intercourse with the Orthodox Russian Church, we by the present message extend to them for the last time the word of admonition and invite them to undertake repentance before the Church, in the knowledge that, as St. John Chrysostom teaches, "to disrupt the unity and fullness of the Church is no less an evil than to foster heresy." This is the final appeal.

Obviously, this appeal would hardly be attractive to the leadership of the Synod, but it did serve one very important purpose: it provided a legal basis by which individual leaders of that orientation could be received back into patriarchal jurisdiction. Nikolai would find this very useful in France.

The Synod possessed only a comparatively small number of parishes in France, however. Metropolitan Evlogii was by far the most important figure among the Russian Orthodox in France, and in late 1944 he had privately sent a letter to the Moscow patriarchate via the Soviet ambassador, in which he expressed a desire to return into the fold of the mother church. He had been invited to the council of 1945, but because of ill health he had not attended.

Evlogii, very old and visibly approaching the end of his life, apparently was sincere in his desire to return to Russian jurisdiction before his death. Regardless of what motivated Evlogii to seek this reunion, and whether or not he had overestimated the significance of the change in religious policy undertaken by the state in 1943, his desire was immensely fortunate for Soviet foreign policy. It offered the possibility of bringing the major part of Russian Orthodoxy in France under the jurisdiction of the Moscow patriarchate and thereby into conformity with Soviet plans for western Europe. The major question, however, was whether the aged and respected Evlogii would be able to bring all of the parishes under his control with him in his return.

It seemed necessary for Nikolai to visit France personally, and he and two priests arrived in Paris on August 24, 1945. His assignment was a difficult one, probably the most difficult he had ever undertaken, for his task was to attempt to bring all the Russian Orthodox in France under the control of Moscow. He apparently did not visit the Soviet Embassy immediately on his arrival, but instead was met at the airport by the Soviet ambassador himself.

Nikolai's meetings with Evlogii went very smoothly, and no problems arose in securing his return to the fold. Curiously enough, no mention of repentance was made; ordinarily the return of a schismatic must be preceded by public repentance and absolution. Evlogii was uncertain about whether his parishes would follow him, however, and asked Nikolai's help in persuading them. Accordingly, a meeting of Evlogii's clergy was held, and in Nikolai's own words:

I gave an address about the relations of Church and state in the Soviet Union, religious freedom, the governmental Council for the Affairs of the Russian Orthodox Church, the patriotic activities of the Church, our institutions for clerical education, monasteries, temples, and the life of our Church in general. And, when I had concluded my speech with the words, "The Russian

Orthodox Church, as a mother, spreads her arms wide and with warm maternal feelings calls all of you, her children, under her wings," at once I felt that these words were long desired, they found a very warm response in the hearts of all those present.[14]

Other evidence suggests that the scene was not quite so idyllic, that there was vigorous opposition. Nevertheless, the outcome was a complete triumph for Nikolai, as Evlogii, his leading prelates, and his entire church were received back into the Muscovite fold.

There was one minor matter that had not been cleared up. Metropolitan Evlogii bore the title of exarch of the Ecumenical Patriarchate, and hence he technically could not seek to return to Muscovite jurisdiction without first obtaining permission from the patriarch at Constantinople. Nikolai, perhaps sensing that it was necessary to move quickly while conditions were favorable, led Evlogii to believe that this had already been taken care of. In fact it had not, as Nikolai certainly knew. His thorough education and demonstrated interest in canon law would surely make him especially sensitive to such a trespass against the jurisdictional rules of Orthodoxy. His failure to make this matter clear during his discussion with Evlogii, and, indeed, his willingness to accept Evlogii back into Muscovite jurisdiction without public repentance, are in clear contrast to his training as a churchman.

Nikolai achieved full success in his dealings with *émigré* Orthodoxy of Evlogii's jurisdiction. His negotiations with the Synod orientation in France were even easier.

The Synod churches in France were led by Metropolitan Serafim, who, because of his blinding hatred for Soviet communism, had supported the Germans even during their occupation of France. According to one of the people present during Nikolai's first meeting with him, Serafim found

Nikolai's proposition quite unacceptable and began questioning Nikolai about the fate of bishops who had remained in the Soviet Union. This, of course, placed Nikolai in a rather embarrassing position.

The second meeting, though, was held in private, and at its conclusion Serafim had decided to accept the offer of returning to Muscovite jurisdiction. This *volte face* on Serafim's part, which directly contradicted his long attitude of vehement opposition to the clerics in Moscow, has elicited the hypothesis that Nikolai's chief argument was simply that, unless Serafim submitted, Nikolai would denounce him as a collaborator with the Germans and have him brought to trial. Feelings about collaborators were still running high in France at that time, and this argument would have been very persuasive indeed.

There was one other aspect to his work, both in France and in England, but here it is difficult to evaluate his success. Nikolai devoted some of his attention to persuading Russian *émigrés* to leave the West and return home. By appealing to homesickness and patriotic yearnings for the Russia of their youth, and by describing in glowing terms the change of heart that allegedly had come over the government, he doubtless was able to be very persuasive. But he certainly could not have been very candid about what would await them on their return.

Even before the war had ended, Stalin's regime was beginning a general tightening of control, which would reach its zenith in the so-called *Zhdanovshchina* of 1947. The basis of Stalinist rule was a closed society, with very little contact with the outside world, and that rigidly under state control. Even Soviet escapees from German prisoner-of-war camps were under suspicion, and some were summarily shot upon their return to Soviet lines, while the vast majority of the rest were sent to labor camps with long sentences.[15] Anyone who had had contact with the West was suspected of contamination. Of course anyone returning after many years abroad would have an uncertain future at best in Stalin's Russia. For Nikolai to attempt to cajole *émigrés* to return to the USSR amounted to persuading them to give up the security and freedom of the West for a future that would be doubtful and possibly tragic.

Not that Nikolai alone was guilty; he was in the company of the United States government as well in this morally questionable activity. One of the less happy pages of America's history was the forcible repatriation of Russian displaced persons immediately after the war.[16] America, however, could claim ignorance, for the Americans apparently felt that only a traitor would not wish to return home, and, in the heady atmosphere of the Soviet-American alliance, applied the same rule to Soviet citizens. The U.S. Army cooperated, sometimes rather brutally, with the Soviet policy of forcible repatriation.

But Nikolai certainly could not claim ignorance of the possible fate awaiting returnees. He knew very well the Soviet attitude toward those "infected" with Western ideas, and because of his intimate knowledge of the inner life of the church and his close contact with the government (and especially the Secret Police), he could not possibly have being ignorant of the state's policy.

A case could be made, however, that the contrast between life in Paris and the USSR was not so great in 1945, especially for that large segment of the Russian emigration that was unable to assimilate into the unfamiliar society and that had adapted poorly to the economic life of the West. Also, if Nikolai were deeply infected with Russian nationalism, it would not be unnatural for his love of the Russian land to be so overpowering as to make it inconceivable that anyone could live away from the homeland.

More important to a patriot, though, is the feeling that if one emigrates he becomes irrelevant to the fate of his country. Russia had experienced cataclysmic difficulties during the war, and the rebuilding of the country would require all the talent available to it. In particular, a churchman would feel a desperate need for Christians during these critical years when the country would be rebuilding and forming into the shape it would have in the future. Christians were a minority movement in the Soviet Union now, and trained churchmen and clerics could be of genuine service.

One vital gift that the *émigrés* could bring on their return would be the gift of theology. There had been no schools in the Russian church for a generation, and the necessities of life had precluded theological development. But the Russian *émigrés* in Paris had achieved worldwide respect for theological studies, and their fresh insight could be of immense service to the Russian church in its continuing competition with communism.[17]

If such motivations were present in Nikolai, there is no mention of them, either in the official report of the visit (where one would not expect to find such comments in any case) or in Western reports of his conduct during the visit. Such motivations certainly played a large role in the decisions of many of those who returned, and provide a basis upon which some of the postwar returns of Russian *émigrés* to the homeland may be justly described as heroic.

All things considered, Nikolai's visit to Paris was a resounding success. He had secured jurisdiction over both branches of Russian Orthodoxy in France, and, in the process, his visit had produced exceedingly good publicity for the

USSR. He was honored by the Soviet Embassy before he left Paris and by the patriarch on his return to Moscow. This triumph, together with his unexpected successful visit to London, demonstrated that Nikolai's skills in the foreign policy of the church were unparalleled.

All would soon prove completely fruitless, however. The expansionist ambitions of Soviet foreign policy would not be masked indefinitely. Even the friendliest observer could not be in doubt long about the effects of Soviet domination of eastern European countries. The enigmatic wartime stance of Stalin was quickly replaced by a vigorous propaganda assault more and more violently anti-Western in its content. The Comintern, whose dissolution in 1941 had been heralded as the death of Communist internationalism, was replaced by the Cominform in 1947, and it quickly became apparent that Soviet foreign policy, as before, was not loathe to employ its subversive arm. Considering how openly Soviet foreign policy showed its hostility to the non-Communist world, it is a wonder that the church was able to retain any of the advantages that it had gained in its foreign activities during and immediately after the war.

The Orthodox churches of the eastern European nations, of course, remained perfectly loyal to the leadership of the Russian church. Certain of the Middle Eastern patriarchs, notably Antioch and, to a lesser extent, Alexandria, also remained on friendly terms, doubtless due in part to gifts and funds they received in return.

The plan to secure for the Moscow patriarchate the position of leadership over all the Orthodox world, however, was completely frustrated. The Ecumenical Patriarch, at Constantinople, had from the first been very hesitant to associate too closely with the Russian church. Any hope of overcoming this reticence and finding some way to persuade him to relinquish, either *de jure* or *de facto*, his position as first among equals was permanently lost when the Soviet state, already involved in border incidents with Iran, began openly to support the Communists in the civil war in Greece. Naturally, this open display of Soviet ambition also removed any possibility of acceptance of Muscovite leadership by the Greek Orthodox Church.

The militance of Soviet foreign policy was also instrumental in frustrating the negotiations of the Moscow patriarchate with Russian Orthodoxy in America. The brief history of postwar contact between the Muscovite and American Orthodox Churches would seem to indicate that it was the inept and heavy hand of the Soviet state, rather than mismanagement by the Russian church, that was responsible for the debacle.

The Russian church in America was much more acclimated to Western life than were the European churches, perhaps because a great number of its members had left Russia well before the Revolution of 1917. Accordingly, it had broken relations with the Synod Abroad because of the Synod's support for the Nazis, and the American church had entered wholeheartedly into the spirit of wartime Soviet-American friendship. With the end of the war, however, it was in a difficult position, for it had no canonical status at all. The continued militant anti-Communism of the Synod made restoration of the prewar affiliation repugnant at that time, so the leader of the Russian church in America appealed to the Moscow patriarch for reinstatement as an autonomous church under Muscovite jurisdiction. This gave to the patriarchate an excellent opportunity to gain control over the entire Russian church of North America.

The patriarchate replied that such a move would, among other things, require an affidavit by the leadership and all the parishes renouncing political expressions against the USSR, and a guarantee to the patriarch of the exclusive right to select the leader of the American church. The patriarchate sent a special envoy, an Archbishop Aleksii, who during his several months in the United States made many enemies by his rather heavy-handed attempts to seize control. Nevertheless, in November 1946, a council at Cleveland, Ohio, voted, over the opposition of many of its leaders, to affiliate with Moscow.

The patriarchate responded by demanding that Veniamin, patriarchal exarch in the United States since 1939, be head of the American church, rather than its elected leader, Feofil. Metropolitan Grigorii was sent to the United States in July 1947, and immediately on arrival presented an ultimatum that Moscow be the sole determinant of the terms of autonomy, and the Grigorii's authority be unquestioned. Shortly thereafter Veniamin was transferred back to the USSR, and Archbishop Makarii, who had uncanonically affiliated with Moscow some months earlier and had been excommunicated by the church in America, was appointed exarch (and hence titular head of the church in America if it should accept Muscovite jurisdiction). Quite naturally, Feofil refused to see Grigorii under these conditions, and there the matter ended.

This certainly seemed a strange form of mismanagement when compared with Nikolai's handling of the French church. No repetition of the 1927 demand of political loyalty was required there, and, since this was the issue that had been the primary cause of the initial rupture, it seems odd that the demand was resurrected for the American church. Nikolai's skill contrasts markedly with the conduct of the delegates sent to the United States, who certainly did not seem the best qualified representatives of Russian Orthodoxy. In Paris, Evlogii was accepted as patriarchal exarch, whereas in the United States a blunt and predictably unacceptable demand was made that a patriarchal appointee be accepted as leader.

Perhaps most significant, the negotiations in Paris were completed with great speed before the favorable political situation had dissipated. The American affair was allowed to drag on until the political mood had shifted and Soviet-American amicability had given way to the Cold War.

On this basis, it would seem that the American affair did not show the smooth, skillful hand of Nikolai, or, indeed, of the church. The church was certainly capable of negotiations with more finesse. Instead, it almost seems as though the MVD had decided to direct the matter itself, and, because of its great lack of expertise in areas outside of normal intelligence and subversion, mismanaged the entire operation.

The hand of the state is even more in evidence in the relations with the Orthodox of France following Nikolai's successful negotiations. Soviet policy in the Middle East, as we have seen, succeeded in confirming the ecumenical patriarch's suspicions about the Soviet Union. No special efforts appear to have been made to gain his agreement to the transfer of French Orthodoxy to Muscovite jurisdiction. On August 8, 1946, Metropolitan Evlogii died. Panic ensued in the Moscow patriarchate, and Metropolitan Grigorii was immediately dispatched to Paris. Normally, Evlogii would have been succeeded by Archbishop Vladimir, his second in command. However, Grigorii insisted that Serafim replace Evlogii. Because Serafim had been of the Synod orientation, he was roundly despised by the other jurisdiction (feelings run especially high between rival groups of *émigré* Russian Orthodox). To the Soviet Secret Police, however, Serafim was doubtless the most favored candidate, because the threat of exposing his past record of collaboration with the Nazis gave them a continuing guarantee of his good conduct. The churches of Evlogii's jurisdiction refused to accept Serafim as their leader, and, because their ties with the Ecumenical Patriarch had not yet been severed, renounced Muscovite affiliation and reverted to their former position. Serafim's usefulness to the Russian church declined rapidly thereafter, and in 1950 he accepted the patriarch's invitation to retire to a monastery near Moscow. Most of his parishes, of course, had reverted back to Synod jurisdiction.

Thus the mismanagement of the French churches succeeded in erasing completely the successes Nikolai had won. It is possible that Nikolai was responsible, but it would be very difficult to explain his adroitness in 1945 in the light of the ineptitude displayed thereafter. Much more likely is the hypothesis that after Nikolai's initial success the MVD took charge, and, again because of its ignorance of such matters, mismanaged the affair completely.

The climax of the Muscovite campaign to gain complete control over the Orthodox world came with the Moscow patriarchate's attempt to call a pan-Orthodox conference in Moscow. Patriarch Aleksii's initial summons to such a conference was frustrated by the Ecumenical Patriarch's refusal on the grounds that only the Ecumenical Patriarch at Constantinople was empowered to convene such a conference. The Russian church then invited all the Orthodox leaders to a celebration of the 500th anniversary of its autocephality, adding that there would be a conference after the ceremonies.

The plan, obviously, was to declare the gathering an Ecumenical Council, for it would have been the first occasion since the seventh century when all the patriarchs had met together. With such a gathering occurring in Moscow at the invitation of the Russian church, the Moscow patriarchate would then have gained the position, *de facto* and possibly *de jure*, of "first among equals." The historical dominance of the Ecumenical Patriarchate would be ended, and all of Orthodoxy would fall under Soviet influence.

To be sure, such a maneuver would hardly be the most

upright manner to gain the position of most respected patriarchate. Had Nikolai been troubled by the morality of the maneuver, however, he could probably have justified it to himself by appealing to the traditional Third Rome doctrine. According to this theory, just as Rome lost its preeminence when the barbarian invasions caused the transfer of the state to Constantinople, so the latter lost its preeminence to Moscow when conquered by the Turks. More to the point was the strong feeling within the Russian church that, because it embraced the largest Orthodox population while the Ecumenical Patriarch had only a few scattered parishes, predominance in the Orthodox world rightly belonged to Moscow.

Such rationalizing was hardly necessary, however. The 1948 celebration failed completely in its aspirations to conciliar authority. The Berlin blockade had begun in June, and by the time the celebration convened the following month it was obvious to all that any gathering in Moscow would necessarily be influenced by the political tension between East and West. The result was that there were a great many absentees.[18] In fact, the council of 1945 had come much closer to representing the Orthodox world than did the celebration of 1948.[19]

The celebration was held, nevertheless, and certain oblique claims to ecumenical status were made, although they had an unmistakably hollow ring. Protestantism and Catholicism were condemned, but the implied juxtaposition of peace-loving Orthodoxy over against war-mongering non-Orthodoxy was so indicative of Soviet policy rather than Orthodox theology that its total effect was quite ludicrous.[20]

Thus, the celebration of 1948 marked the total collapse of the grand design to which Stalin, Aleksii, and Nikolai had agreed in 1945. The only successes that endured were in eastern Europe, where the presence of the Red Army guaranteed success, and in the minuscule Russian colony in Manchuria, which was caught between Soviet might on the one side and the victorious Chinese Communists on the other. In Middle Eastern Orthodoxy (notably at Antioch), there remained some friendliness to Moscow, but one suspects that this was not viewed as an unmixed blessing by the Soviet state, for this friendliness was retained at the cost of considerable subsidies.

Orthodoxy in western Europe had slipped from the grasp of Soviet control, and was becoming as embarrassingly anti-Communist as before. Great Britain was no longer neutralized. Russian Orthodoxy in America was beginning to align itself with the prevailing mood of the United States, which had quickly become the chief obstacle to further Soviet expansion. The foreign policy of the Russian Orthodox Church was at a low ebb. Nikolai's career was probably also at a low ebb.

But perhaps it was not. Nikolai had achieved considerable success in the matters he had attended to personally. He had convincingly demonstrated his great ability in foreign affairs. His work had come to naught, apparently, only after his direction had been replaced by that of the Soviet Secret Police.

There was still one part of his work that had not been taken over by the MVD. The MVD could not imitate those individual capabilities that Nikolai had brought to his task: the personal winsomeness, the poise, the tact—in short, the image that Nikolai was able to create. The value that remained out of all of Nikolai's efforts was the lasting friendliness he had won for the USSR, in England and elsewhere, through his own, particular, highly personalized approach to propaganda.

V

The Pastor: Sin and the
Christian Life

S o far we have been considering Metropolitan Nikolai's public life as a high prelate of the church. There was another side of Nikolai, which presents a radically different picture. Nikolai was a regular contributor of sermons and messages in the *Journal of the Moscow Patriarchate*, which he edited. Another Nikolai emerges in these sermons, most of which were delivered in the course of his liturgical duties in various Russian cathedrals. Prepared primarily for an audience of worshipers, these sermons display none of the suave urbanity of the politician of the church. Instead they suggest a Russian pastor extraordinarily gifted in public speaking and deeply thoughtful about the meaning of his faith.

Nikolai was not a speculative theologian. Whatever his talents may have been, theological erudition was not one of them. But this is not to say that his sermons are unconcerned about the deeper meanings of the Christian faith, untouched by the inward dimension of the Christian life.

Russian Orthodoxy as a whole has not been much inclined

to logical development of the doctrine of the church. Few indeed are the really first-rate theologians that the Russian church has produced. The intellectual element in Russian Orthodoxy has always taken second place to the mystical. The mystical, inward, spiritually oriented aspects of the "Russian soul" doubtless derive in large measure from the deep identification of Orthodoxy with the Russian people. Life is a divine mystery to the Orthodox, ever lived more in the realm of the spirit than of the flesh. The Russian people have never been as able as Westerners to concentrate on the material aspects of life to the exclusion of the spiritual. Thus Russian Orthodoxy is a highly contemplative, rather than a predominantly rational, approach to Christianity.[1]

The great appeal of the church in this century has been among people who are forty or older. While the pressures of Soviet antireligious policy doubtless contribute to the relative lack of young people in the churches,[2] it may also be that the deeply contemplative approach to religion is much more appealing to those whose youthful ideals and enthusiasms have run their course. Perhaps the ultimate introspective questions—the questions of death and eternity—are more meaningful to those for whom memory has begun to supplant ambition.[3]

Precisely because Russian Orthodoxy is a deeply contemplative form of Christianity, more concerned with ultimate matters than with the practical trivia of daily life, pietism is a very common feature among Orthodox people. Because pietism concentrates so intensely on the inner, devotional life, perhaps it is understandable that one of the besetting failings of the pietist is an incomplete application of the tenets of the devotional life to the outer life of action. Doubtless this compartmentalization of religion is not nearly so common among pietists as is generally assumed, and in

Soviet conditions, the restriction of permissible church activity exclusively to worship intensifies this tendency. But
the temptation to a compartmented faith is always present,
and a deeply devotional, inward, pietistic habit of faith could
lead toward an unconscious compartmentalization of life. It
is always difficult to apply one's beliefs fully amidst the rush
of activity in life, and Russian Orthodoxy would seem much
more prone to the temptation to isolate the private life of
the devotional from day-to-day activities than might some
other forms of the Christian faith.

Particularly in the life of Nikolai would there be difficulty
in bridging with perfect consistency the brutally political
world of the Communist state with the mystical, devotional
world of the Orthodox liturgy. So it is not really surprising
to observe in Nikolai's sermons a tendency to regard the
Christian religion as a haven, a place of eternity's security to
which the distraught soul can repair.

Thus does our soul in our innermost lives, hidden from the
view of others, seek cleanness and fresh air for itself. It has to
live and breathe in an atmosphere drunk with the miasma of
human sins, suffering, reciprocal evils, lies, and places of all the
moral sins. . . . For this do we come hither into God's temple,
leaving at the threshold of this temple all our fuss, all our cares,
all that by which we anxiously live in this world. Here we
breathe another atmosphere.[4]

Unquestionably, modern political life is not especially
kind to the person who tries to regulate his life by norms
other than expedient practicality. Regardless of how sincerely he strives for consistency in his life, his actions will
sometimes fall short of that Christian ideal he wishes to follow. For someone with the pietistic inclinations that Nikolai's
sermons display, there will always be an inclination to prefer

the lucidity of the devotional life to the compromising realities of life in the world.

On this [earthly] path Faith serves him as that Rock on
which he stands, and he does not fear the storms and trials of
life. The Church is for him that native home under whose roof
he always finds warmth and peace for himself. In the person of
the Mother of God he finds for himself a heavenly mother to
whom he can always in prayer tell everything which gladdens
or depresses his spirit. He lives by the hope that the Heavenly
Father, always true to His promise, will give to him in the life
of the future age the joy to be a participant in eternal blessedness.

And inspired by these holy joys of his faith, the Christian
in his soul adheres ever more closely to God and in fellowship
with Him lives in true happiness.[5]

This was the ideal of life expressed in Nikolai's sermons.
The Christian life was one saturated with a sense of mystical
fellowship with God, a life whose worth was to be measured
not by the accomplishments and achievements of this world,
or even by the realization of Christian ideals in this world,
but by the inner life of the individual Christian, by the
degree to which the presence of God was felt in the person's
life.

The burden of Christ is a light burden, according to the
inerrant word of the Father. Why? Because none of us whom
He calls to take His yoke upon us is left alone by Him in bearing this yoke. The Lord surrounds us on all the paths of our
life with His help, with that of His Mother, of all the saints to
whom we sigh with our hearts. . . . Oh, we are rich in the
help of Heaven, and thousands of invisible hands are extended
to us from thence, to uphold us, to strengthen us, to lead us
thither, to lighten the cross and labors of life for the salvation
of our soul and for the Kingdom of God.

. . . But [this labor] fulfills the commandments of God—

everyone is able, for everyone it is easy and light, because it consists of just that which our nature demands: mercy, pardon, physical and spiritual cleanliness, lack of wrath, righteousness—yes, every living soul wants to live and breathe by these! But lying, spite, anger, wrath—these are foreign to our spirit, they contradict our spirit, as that which befouls and stains it. Each of us is well acquainted with the torments of our accusing conscience after such sins.[6]

It is interesting that immorality and sin are evaluated in the light of the inner, devotional relationship to God. Immoral actions interrupt one's inner fellowship with God. Such actions are not evaluated in terms of their intrinsic evil, nor, apparently, is the guilt that follows their commission due to the objective reprehensibility of the actions. Sinful acts are to be avoided not so much because they contradict the law of God or the requirements of Christian morality, but because they interfere with the inward peace of one's devotional relationship to God.

Nikolai's sermons have none of that insensitivity to evil that some of his public activities might suggest. His sermons persistently return to the problem of evil, but, almost without exception, their approach to the problem is in exclusively devotional terms. The social and public effects of evil, the forensic demands of righteousness, even the suffering that evil actions create for others have been overshadowed completely by devotional considerations.

The Savior told us that no one is able to take this joy from us—neither suffering, nor sickness, nor people, nor the thought of death, nor death itself can take this joy from him who has acquired it in his heart.

Only one thing can take it away from us—sin. When sin enters into a person's heart and rules that heart, no longer can the Spirit of God be in it, for "what communion hath light with darkness?" (II Cor. 6:14) says the holy Apostle Paul. "There is no joy for the dishonorable," says the Word of God.

Sin which is unrecognized and therefore unmourned and unexpiated, especially sin which is persistent and of long duration, breaks the human soul's link with God. It drives out of the heart thanksgiving, the spirit of prayer—all that by which this heart lived until its enslavement to sin. And in addition it deprives it of that joy in God which this heart possessed earlier.

Let each of us not only in his thought but in all his being recognize that our most terrible enemy is sin. Let each of us not begrudge the labors which sometimes are even very grievous in order to drive out of the heart both the fruits and the root itself of sin and sufferings.[7]

Nikolai's sermons present the devotional life of the Christian in terms of struggle. His was not a theology that ignores the tension of the life of faith. Evil is a powerful force in life, one requiring vigorous and continual resistance. Nikolai's sermons do not advocate "nonresistance to evil," at least not in one's devotional life.

In the person of the apostle Timothy, the apostle Paul addresses himself to all of us as well. He calls all of us "good soldiers" and says that we should "fight." If we are soldiers that means that we have an enemy with whom we do battle and of course there are enemies: not external but internal. For we are not ordinary soldiers but soldiers of Jesus Christ. If we are soldiers, then we should have arms, and of course not external but internal, as the apostle Paul says in the epistle to the Corinthians: "For the weapons of our warfare are not carnal." (II Cor. 10:5)

Who are these enemies with whom we should do battle as good soldiers? It is first of all sin. . . .

Battle with this enemy is difficult because in addition he never falls on us alone: One sin always brings another behind it. It is enough for a man to enter on the path of lying, for criticism and slander and spite to rise in his heart. All these sins are interconnected with a single chain.[8]

Here and there in Nikolai's sermons, talk of evil brings a note of pessimism. The life of the spirit is one of joy and victory, yet the power of evil is so great that sometimes he seems to wonder if it can be overcome. A hint of dejection, of sorrow creeps into his treatment of sin, almost a lamentation. Nikolai's life had not been an easy one, and, doubtless, in his rise to a position of leadership in the church he had more than the normal share of temptations to fall, consciously or unconsciously, from the ideals of the devotional life. Even in sermons written long before his death, while he was yet in the prime of middle age, there often appeared a note of that dejection, that trace of bitterness and despair that might appear as an old man at the conclusion of life looks back and surveys the errors and sins, the opportunities missed and now forever lost.

And each of us from childhood became adolescents and from adolescence, young people. And how clean, how undepravedly clean, was the spirit of each of us in childhood. Can the heart remember this without unrest? In childhood we did not know how to lie, nor did we know abusive words, nor did we bear in ourselves envy or evil; in our activities we were like angels. The Lord, the Savior, says, "Except ye be converted and become as little children ye shall not enter into the Kingdom of Heaven." (Matt. 18.3) The clean spirit of a child is worthy of the heavenly kingdom.

And lo, gradually the childlike soul begins to be defiled; the first lying word falls from the mouth, the blush of shame suffuses the face of the youngster when for the first time he tells a lie. He begins to recognize envy, jealousy; depraved surroundings begin to push him into other vices. At first the spirit conceals as it were a film of sin, scarcely visible to the spiritual eye; then when a man becomes accustomed to sin, sin begins to adhere to the immortal soul with whole layers of its filth.

· · ·

And before the Lord Himself sums up the earthly life of each of us, many times on the path of our lives we should turn back to the life we have lived and always see before us its totality. And if only we turn back and look at what each of us has lived through—and many of us are already drawing near to the limit of our earthly life—how many of our mistakes will we see, our fallings, how many sins will we find in our past, not only unrepented and unatoned but even unrecognized and forgotten! We shall not see "fruit worthy of repentance," as we ought to bring for the atonement of our sins. Our great misfortune is that we do not know, do not feel the passing of life, that we do not fulfill the wisdom and holiness of the apostolic admonition, "redeeming the time for the days evil." (Eph. 5:16) The days are evil because they are like swiftly flowing water: as the river bears its waters to the seas and oceans and as the oceans never return them to their sources, so the days and years of our lives falling into the ocean of eternity never return to man. That which has gone by will never return. Doubtless many among us are people who passionately, fervently want to start life again in order not to repeat the mistakes they have made, in order not to give a place in their hearts to those vices and passions which we have gotten used to, in order to live otherwise. But life gives to us only one time, and each of its years, each of its days, and each hour should be pricelessly dear to us.

. . . Each of us is drawing near to the inevitable end of our earthly path. Not only should we, the people who are not far from the end of life, be aware of it, but also the people who are only setting out along life's path. Because none of us knows the time of the boundary of life, one has to be prepared for death, and the earlier we begin this, the greater will be the peace and spiritual calm with which we think on death, and the greater will be the joy with which we await our life with Christ in the endless ages.[9]

The great danger of falling into evil lies in the cumulative power of evil. For the introspective Christian, whose religious life is primarily devotional, the deadening power such lapses have over the spiritual life is an acute danger. Devotional life requires a certain purity of spirit, and if evil has broken the link with the divine, if the crystal clarity of the mystical relationship has become clouded, the believer wanders in a desert of spiritual deadness, and the restoration of his religious life is difficult indeed. Evil is habit-forming.

And all sinners who are filthy with their grave sins are like travellers who have lost their way on a snowy night. Sins blind our spiritual vision; sins bind our hands and feet in the spiritual sense. Isolated by terrors and entangled in sins we often lose the very path to repentance: we know not how to recognize our sins, nor to understand their destructive power, nor to find in ourselves the decisiveness and daring to go to God with repentance. Often we do not have the power to be inspired with faith and hope in the mercy of God.[10]

The only cure for such a condition, then, is repentance. Repentance, the inner act of turning from evil to God, is the chief antidote for sin, for it is only by repentance that the inward relationship to God can be restored. Nikolai's sermons mention the outward concommitant of repentance, expiation, relatively infrequently. To make restitution, to right the wrong done by the evil action, to renounce decisively the repetition of the error in one's daily life—all are overshadowed by the inner act of repentance. Because it concentrates on the inward, rather than the social or public, aspects of the faith, pietism is often very strong in its emphasis on repentance and relatively weak in its attention to rectification of the wrong. Perhaps the sacrament of Confession contributes to this imbalance somewhat, for the penance prescribed often is in the form of additional devotional exercise.

For the Christian who is seeking eternal salvation there should be repentance for his sins and tears about his sins—not only when we stand before the priest and open our soul before him. This repentance is an integral property of the believing soul for all the days of the earthly life of a person.

Just as soon as the Christian begins consciously to ponder over his life, he cannot but see the countless blessings and mercies of his Heavenly Father toward him. He knows that all his life from the beginning—from the day of his birth and to his last breath—is in the hands of the loving Heavenly Father, by Whose will this life begins and ends. In the heart of the Christian the feeling of thankfulness, of thankful love to his Father, glows and spreads.[11]

Evil disrupts the developed life of the Christian, breaks the mystical fellowship with God, and, unless it is forcibly resisted, threatens to blind him completely to the spiritual dimension of life. The only cure is repentance. But there is more, much more, to the Christian life than the struggle against evil in one's spiritual life.

The Christian life, as it appears in Nikolai's sermons, is a life of joy and spiritual depth, a life of inward delight in God, of secret communion with Him. The Christian life is serene, perfectly secure against the intrusions of the evil world surrounding it, a life whose spiritual dimension engulfs all the trivial nuisances of earthly life in the aura of eternity. It is a life of delicious, inexpressible, inexhaustible peace.

And the peace brought to the earth by the Lord Jesus Christ does not dwell on the earth. The Lord predicted for the earth even these wars of people against people, kingdom with kingdom (Matt. 24:7), and these tribulations which are inevitable in the earthly life of each person: "In the world ye shall have tribulation." (John 16:33) But he also said to us: "My kingdom is not of this world," (John 18:36) and again: "The Kingdom of God is within you." (Luke 17:21)

The peace of Christ is one of the properties of the Kingdom

of God and dwells where the Kingdom of God stays: within us, in our heart, in each true Christian soul.

The peace given by the Savior to mankind is first of all peace with God, the peace of the soul which is devoted to the Lord and which loves Him. It lives in that heart in which there is no murmur against God, which accepts everything that happens in life as from the hand of God, with full trust, with complete filial obedience, as the will of its Heavenly Father. "Have Thy way with me, Lord," is the voice of the clean heart. This peace is worthy of that soul which is drunk with grateful love to its Lord for all the numberless blessings of God, a love completely foreign to dry—even more, black—criminal thanklessness to its God like that of the Judeans. This peace will not be in the soul when a person who has fallen into sin wants to convince himself that if these sins are hidden from people they are also hidden from almighty God, or when, having given himself over to sin with lightness of spirit, he lulls his conscience with the idea that the Lord, according to His mercy, will forgive even without repentance of the sin and in no case will condemn. . . .

The peace of Christ is the peace of the Christian spirit in relation to its neighbors. It is the treasure of that one who does not hold in his bosom a stone against his neighbor, who does not bear in himself either a thirst for personal place or personal hatred, or memory of offenses caused him; in whose heart does not dwell a spirit of condemnation, envy, jealousy, or boasting. . . .

. . . To strive to acquire this peace means to strive that the Lord move into the heart and live in it in accordance with His promise (John 14:23); it means to make our heart a temple of the Holy Spirit dwelling in us (I Cor. 6:19), and, carefully keeping this priceless treasure in ourself, to enjoy the fruits of the Spirit of God inhabiting us—joy and peace.[12]

Nikolai would have a great deal more to say about peace in the course of his public duties for the church.

VI

The Propaganda

THE POSTWAR SOVIET foreign policy phase of direct expansion had all but run its course by 1948. The situation in western Europe appeared to have stabilized sufficiently to discourage hopes for further expansion in Europe. The harshness of Soviet policies in eastern Europe, the aggressiveness of Soviet actions in the Middle East, and the strident voice of anti-Western propaganda had quickly dissipated what remained of the wartime friendship with the West. The unexpectedly stern Western response to the Berlin blockade gave vivid demonstration to the fact that the time of expansion had come to a close and a new direction would have to be found for Soviet foreign policy.

The Berlin debacle resulted in a complete abandonment of previous tendencies toward disarmament in the United States, and the Soviet Union quickly found itself faced with the unpleasant prospect of a revitalized and determinedly anti-Communist adversary possessing a vast and vigorous economy, naval and strategic air superiority, and a monopoly of atomic weapons. Before the USSR could hope to challenge such competition, time would be required to allow the Soviet economy to grow and to develop its nuclear weapons program. Thus, Soviet foreign policy was forced to shift its strategy from aggressive expansion to a primarily defensive stance, the major task of which would be to frustrate the attempts of the West to rearm and form military alliances.

The crisis of foreign policy was even more acute in the Russian Orthodox Church in 1948. The grand scheme for cooperative assistance to the expansion of Soviet domination had come to naught. In spite of the good beginnings, the church had been unable to acquire lasting control in western Europe, Great Britain, and the United States. The only lasting successes were in the Middle East, and in eastern Europe where the presence of the Red Army guaranteed ecclesiastical good behavior.

It seemed fairly obvious that the services of the church were no longer so essential to Soviet foreign policy as they had seemed to be in 1945. Soviet cash and the power of the Red Army would doubtless continue to be effective with or without the active cooperation of church officials in Moscow. With the total collapse of the church's hopes for vast influence in the international sphere, the profitability of the church's services declined precipitately. In 1948 it appeared that the state could well afford to treat the church's collaboration with indifference.

This spelled potential disaster for the church. The church's ability to bargain with the state had saved it from complete destruction when the crisis of war had made the church's standing offer of political collaboration attractive to the state. The concessions won by the church in 1943 had been a form of payment for its services to the state in the war effort. Similarly, the continuation of those concessions after the war was probably permitted by the state in return for the church's collaboration in the regime's foreign policy. If such political collaboration was no longer profitable to the state, the church could scarcely hope to retain the concessions.

These concessions were still essential to the church's continued survival in the USSR. The process of rebuilding within the church was far from complete. Some churches had been reopened, but the number was still far from adequate.[1] The complement of bishops had been increased to about seventy, but that was still less than half the number that had been active in 1930, and many sees were vacant.[2] The ranks of the priesthood were still very thin, with most parishes occupied by priests well past retirement age, and it would be many years before the newly opened seminaries could begin to meet the need. The church had made great strides in its recovery, but in 1948 it was still far short of a truly healthy condition.

The growing intrenchment of Stalin's regime as it continued to tighten its control over the Russian countryside was increasingly ominous. Zhdanov, who was identified with the increased severity of totalitarian controls, was in the ascendancy in 1948, and his death in August of that year resulted in no appreciable amelioration of the rigor of Soviet rule. In the past, every increase in the severity of Soviet control over society had fallen with especial vigor on the church, and the church's somber history of decline is particularly marked in these periods of increased severity in the regime's relationship to society at large.[3] Whether or not Russian Orthodoxy had begun to feel a renewal of the antireligious campaign in 1948, stern repression of illegal religions by the police was well underway,[4] and in view of this the Orthodox church could only wonder how long it would be before the campaign would expand to include it also.

For this reason, the failure of the church's foreign policy was probably felt especially keenly in the patriarchate, for it meant a loss of the crucial bargaining point. It was imperative that the church find some alternative way to be of political service to the state.

Fortunately, an area of service was beginning to develop in 1948, one that would allow Nikolai to continue to assist the state in foreign affairs.

As we have seen, the single area in which Nikolai's work had not been frustrated by the ineptitude of state practitioners of foreign policy had been in the area of propaganda. Nikolai had demonstrated his considerable abilities as a propagandist for Soviet interests, and the benevolent image he had created for the state in England and France had some lasting effect among the Christians there. Surely his services as a propagandist could continue to be valuable for the state.

It was Soviet exploitation of the peace issue that was to provide Nikolai with the opportunity to be of continued service to the interests of Soviet foreign policy.

The great desire for peace that was sweeping the world in the late forties was by no means a Soviet invention. The horrors of the war, still fresh in the minds of most of the world's population, and the growing tension of the Cold War resulted in a widespread, almost universal, yearning for peace, a yearning that in its fundamental terms was quite without regard to the political aims of one side or the other. It was this all but unspoken desire to have done with war, unquestionably genuine, sincere, and without political origins, that provided the basic conditions on which the Soviet Union could seek to build a relatively sophisticated, remarkably successful instrument for implementing its foreign policy. Because desire for peace and antipathy toward war have been an important aspect of Christianity, this was an area ideally suited to cooperation between the Russian church and the Soviet state.

Pacifism has a long and honorable history in modern Christianity. Every conflict of recent times has elicited protest from a body of Christian clerics and laymen who are of a deep and abiding conviction that the carnage of armed hostility is absolutely irreconcilable with the Christian gospel. The sincerity of that conviction and the honor, commitment, and often the heroism of the protests coming from it can not be impugned. If there have been occasions on which the protests of Christian pacifists have redounded to the benefit of unworthy causes, or if Machiavellian forces have sought to twist pacifistic sentiments to their own uses, it would be a massive injustice to attribute such unfortunate results to pacifism as such, or to question the integrity and honor of the overwhelming majority of the pacifists themselves.

Soviet attempts to mobilize pacifist sentiment to its own ends must be carefully distinguished from that larger desire for peace that was extant in the postwar period. The mere fact that the great publicity given to Soviet entries in the peace field tended to draw attention away from the great bulk of proponents of peace during the years following 1948 should not lead one to the conclusion that the peace movement as a whole displayed the same onesidedness and bias that marked the Soviet-dominated bodies. In order to honor this distinction, the treatment that follows will use the term "PEACE CAMPAIGN" when referring to those several peace organizations (chief of which was the World Peace Council) whose primary role was to serve the interests of Soviet policy, in contrast to the numerically larger body of less publicized pacifist bodies in the peace movement whose activities were not designed to support one side or the other, but rather expressed an honorable and sincere devotion to the larger cause of peace itself.

Early in 1948 the first of the gatherings of the PEACE CAMPAIGN occurred in Wroclaw, Poland, where the idea of forming a special movement for peace was adopted. This idea met with considerable enthusiasm, and similar meetings were organized almost simultaneously in New York and a short time later in Paris. The Soviet leadership was very quick to recognize their potential, and for the next several years the PEACE CAMPAIGN was an important arm of Soviet foreign policy. Especially inasmuch as Soviet foreign policy in the late forties was obliged to take a defensive position until the unfavorable balance of power could be rectified, the PEACE CAMPAIGN became an exceedingly effective means for attempting to frustrate Western desires for rearmament and military alliances.

The great virtue of the PEACE CAMPAIGN was that it could involve non-Communists as well as Communists.[5] Because of its single theme, the PEACE CAMPAIGN could achieve a working alliance of all sorts of people who might be in disagreement on every point but aversion to war. The USSR maintained control of the PEACE CAMPAIGN, and through it was able to enlist broad support for its foreign policy goals of frustrating the growth of Western military strength.

Inasmuch as participation in the PEACE CAMPAIGN did not require acceptance of Party doctrine, and especially inasmuch as the movement sought the widest possible support, it provided an ideal sphere in which the collaboration of the church could be useful to the state. Nikolai rapidly became deeply involved in the peace movement, and for the next several years he was one of its staunchest supporters, adding the implied endorsement of Christianity to the propaganda produced by the PEACE CAMPAIGN in support of particular aspects of Soviet foreign policy.

Nikolai was exceedingly competent in public speaking, and was able to adapt his style fully to the requirements of Soviet propaganda. He gave no evidence of difficulty in conforming to the continually changing emphases required by Soviet interests. His approach and style were remarkably faithful to the traditions of Soviet propaganda, both in general tone and in use of the specific clichés that were the trademark of the Communist practitioners of the art. So great was the impact of his work in the peace movement that his speech at the First USSR Conference for Peace in Moscow (August 1949) was noticed even by the Western press. Nikolai's ability to accommodate himself to the norms of Soviet propaganda is especially evident in the following extract from that speech:

And thus, at a time when our country and the People's Democracies are engaged in peaceful construction and are bending all their will and effort in that direction, common people the world over are alarmed by the ring of a knife, rusty with human blood, as it is sharpened by the hand of a murderer. Death is again raising its ruthless scythe over the fields of the earth, preparing to reap a bountiful harvest. The same dark forces that ten years ago hurled humanity into the abyss of indescribable suffering, again wish to hold a blood feast, for, being born to feed on human blood, they cannot live without it. . . .

The transatlantic octopus is trying to fasten its greedy tentacles around the whole globe. Capitalist America, the rabid fornicatress of resurrected Babylon, having set up a world market, is trying to seduce the people of the world while pushing them toward war. But the common people of all countries are turning their eyes away from her shameless nakedness with a feeling of abomination. None of them are, or can be, enticed. Only those succumb to seduction, who barter away their country and who, in all justice, can be called nothing but sworn enemies of their people.

The transatlantic sirens sing of "liberty." But only a man with a black conscience and a clouded intellect can say that liberty exists in a country where people are lynched, where children are kidnapped, where tear [gas] bombs are thrown at workers, that is, at the people who create the country's wealth, where grain is burned in the sight of the hungry, where those who endeavour to restore to the word "liberty" its true meaning are flung into jail, where gold is minted for the purchase of accomplices in other countries and guns are cast in order to drench in human blood the peaceful valleys of Greece, China, Indonesia and Viet-Nam. Liberty to rob, coerce and slaughter—such is their "liberty"!

The reek of fires, the stench of decaying corpses and the panic fear of the detected criminal are wafted from the camp of the "Western democrats." These people have lost not only conscience, but reason too. They have gone so far in their insanity as to say, with our country directly in mind: "We do not put armies of young men out to gut one another. We send planes over at forty thousand feet loaded with atom bombs, fire bombs and germ bombs to slaughter babies in the cradle, grandmothers at their prayers and working men at their jobs." (*Times Herald*, Washington, July 4, 1949.)

To what depths of depravity, to what spiritual decadence, to what sadistic cynicism, to what weakness born of fear must a man have sunk to pronounce words like these! It is not merely beastly, because a beast, having had his fill, lies down and becomes quiet. The voracity of the present-day cannibals has no bounds. The merchants in human blood, the manufacturers of death, sitting on bags of gold, would be quite ready to exterminate not only the two-hundred-million Soviet population, but all people in general who have the nerve to protest against being killed, leaving for themselves only a small tribe of mute slaves, similar to the slaves of Egypt in the days of the Pharaohs.

Can the Russian Orthodox Church leave without reply such heinous words coming from the cannibals? Can She fail to denounce such an ideology, which wiping out the almost two-thousand-year history of Christian teaching, is nothing but a cry from the pit of hell, the voice of an Antichrist? No, She cannot. She has no right to do so. . . .

"We do not put armies of young men out to gut one another"—shouts the Washington Cain, and in his cry the frenzy of a villain blends with the despair of a coward. Oh, how anxious Cain is to see these millions of young men again hurl themselves against one another in a bloody carnage of self-extermination. But he is aware of the fact that in the family of mankind he, the fratricide, has been exposed and doomed, and that this time the weapons handed out to young men will be turned against him. And so, being powerless to commit his crime, he storms and threatens everyone with the Beast of the Apocalypse, with all the horrors pictured by the delirious imagination of a raving madman.

But all this was already manifested in the recent years of war. There was falsehood and delirium, and lechery and seduction and threat. And after all that, there was one thing more—punishment. . . .

The Russian Orthodox Church considers it a sacred duty to expose from this lofty rostrum all those wolves in sheep's clothing, who hide under high Christian titles, and to open the eyes of the common pious people the world over, the eyes of all believers of the Christian faith, to the abyss of moral savageness, to the chasm of spiritual and physical annihilation into which they are being pushed by those ranking "ecclesiastical leaders."

It is our Christian duty to thus warn, before it is too late, the many thousands of upright Catholic and Protestant priests and pastors and the many millions of the simple believers who comprise their congregations, and to turn to them with our ardent fraternal appeal to resist Cain's temptation of fratricide and to make every effort to strengthen the pious cause of peace.[6]

At first glance, it seems strange to meet that unrestrained invective, that stridency of tone, and that outrage, which one would more naturally associate with wartime propaganda, at a gathering in defense of peace. Indeed, many of Nikolai's peace speeches are distinctly reminiscent of his wartime orations, bearing some of the same vindictiveness which he had employed so fluently then.

Together with all honest men and women the world over the Soviet people declare to the warmongers, to the Anglo-American leaders of imperialist reaction: Our will for peace is indomitable; together with all the peoples that march in our ranks we shall staunchly and selflessly fight for peace till we win: Awful shall be the wrath and ruthless the punishment if you dare to violate the peace won at such a great cost![7]

Thus, the new context into which Nikolai's activities in foreign affairs led him after 1948 did not represent a complete break with his past. He was able to bring to the new task his already familiar habits of vocabulary and style. More importantly, the new requirements of the peace propaganda were by no means completely inconsistent with his life-long vocation as a pastor of the Christian church. In many respects the struggle for peace and against war was perfectly compatible with the deep stream of pietism that is so evident in his sermons.

Each true follower of Christ knows that that same struggle goes on in the world which takes place uninterruptedly in his soul: the struggle between light and darkness, between striving for unity and wholeness and staying in disunity and alienation. Therefore, when he conquers darkness and death in himself, the Christian increases for himself the powers of life and good-

ness in the world, he becomes the ally and aid of all who struggle for truth and peace among peoples. The outcome of this
struggle takes shape within man also, and therefore is participation in it so important for each Christian soul.[8]

Nikolai was able to give a convincing exposition of a
Christian view of the dynamics of the struggle for international peace, especially in his more irenic moments:

But first it is necessary to conquer the temptation to war in
the depths of the individual spirit where the moral stimuli of
human activity and action arise. It is necessary to exclude war
forever from the means of struggle with those who think otherwise than we. It is necessary for all Christians who, to the
present time, have taken a position of reticence, and in many
cases of temporizing and even hostility, toward our movement
to understand at last that one must not distort the childishly
simple teaching of Christ, which is understandable to all and
clear as crystal, by virtue of which there cannot be Christian
aggressive war, Christian murder is unthinkable, and force in
the name of alleged preservation of Christian civilization is
impossible.[9]

It would not appear that Nikolai was presenting these
thoughts as a general philosophy, a serious and objective attempt to delve into the meaning of peace (had he been so
doing, he might have noticed the direct contradiction of his
final statement in the paragraph last quoted with his wartime position, in which he vigorously supported the use of
force for the preservation of Russian culture). Despite the
appearance of having a Christian point of view, these passages in his peace speeches remain primarily propagandistic,
for Nikolai turns to the Christian justification of his peace
activities only in connection with attempts to persuade other
Christians to join the campaign. One of the chief services
his participation could render to the aims of Soviet foreign

policy, of course, was to influence other Christians, especially in the West, to cooperate with the PEACE CAMPAIGN, thus increasing the breadth of the movement and augmenting its usefulness.

It would be most unwise (and perhaps unfair as well) to treat such statements as indicative of Nikolai's own inner reaction to the PEACE CAMPAIGN. Because these statements are designed to accomplish a specific purpose, there is no way of determining the degree to which they were Nikolai's honest exposition of his own feelings about the matter. For Nikolai's first duty in these statements was to appeal for increased participation in the campaign. The following passage, for example, which is one of the better illustrations of Nikolai's ability to enlist the support of Christian theology in his peace propaganda, immediately followed a call to widespread Christian participation in the PEACE CAMPAIGN.

As if to cheer thirsters after Truth, the prophet of the Old Testament said: "And the work of righteousness shall be peace; and the effect of righteousness, quietness and assurance for ever." (Isa. 32:17) Hence, peace issues from the Truth of man's works. God gave man life not for war, but that he might flourish peacefully in mutual love. The spirit of all Holy Scripture testifies that war is not a primordial and natural phenomenon in the race of man, as some maintain to this day (following the heathen philosopher Plato), but is a scourge and an evil brought about by man's licentious digression from the ideal, that is, the fall into sin. We are now against war because we ourselves created it.

The whole service of Christ on earth was a confirmation of the commandment to love and a radiant example of a new life in this love. Christ exhorted His disciples to peace and conciliation and exalted the cause of peacemaking into a Christian virtue.

The apostolic call to follow after the things which make for peace (Rom. 14:19) reiterated the basic principle of Christianity as a religion of love and peace.

Christians, does not this immutable foundation of Christianity impose on us a moral responsibility for the fate of the modern world and of mankind?

The Christian believer will not, of course, justify his inactivity by the argument that since the time of Christ mankind has never ceased to suffer from wars. No, wars did not cease with the coming of Christianity, but on the other hand the conviction that they were necessary and inevitable ceased, and the light of Eternal Peace was kindled in the heart of man. Is this not a sign of coming victory, is it not this light that now beckons all mankind towards peace?

Donning the whole armour of faith we Christians must preach together: war is contrary to Christ's teaching, which we preach, war evokes enmity and defies love, war means violence, which is condemned by Christian freedom, war sets at naught the personality of man, formed in the image and likeness of God![10]

One of the most powerful themes that Nikolai as a representative of the church was able to draw upon was the innate desire of other Christians to have done with the suspicion and distrust that were so much in evidence in international affairs.

Because Nikolai, better than any other Soviet luminary of the PEACE CAMPAIGN, was able to claim sincerity and lack of guile, he was able to be of immense service to the credibility of the movement and, consequently, to its effectiveness in gaining acceptance of Soviet-sponsored policies in international politics.

It is necessary by all means to cleanse the peace for which we are all struggling now from mistrust and insincerity, to elevate it with mutual understanding and friendship, to warm up our inner Christian attitude so that it may become indeed the consequence of the Peace of Christ which we Christians preach.

I wish to say that my Western brothers should widen their view to the positive possibilities of conciliation of peoples, and I fervently call them to strengthen these possibilities by their faith, their preaching, their influence!

We Christians all believe in Peace eternal, unlimited, and at the same time we all wish to utilize peace here on earth—not internal peace only but also external [peace] that is social and international.[10]

The peace issue in many ways was ideally suited for church-state collaboration, for it presented an area in which there was ample room for justification of Christian interest and participation in an activity undertaken by the non-Christian state. Nikolai was thus able to be of genuine service to the state. Much more important, however, was the service that Nikolai's collaboration with the state rendered to the church. The virtual isolation of Russian Orthodoxy internationally had come perilously close to invalidating the bargaining situation, which was the church's only visible means of survival. Nikolai's enthusiastic entry into the PEACE CAMPAIGN revitalized the bargaining situation, for the state could not afford to withdraw the concessions it had granted the church because Nikolai's services, even though they were peripheral to the campaign, were of value to Soviet foreign policy.

The major problem was precisely that Nikolai's services were peripheral. The PEACE CAMPAIGN would continue to serve Soviet international interests whether or not Nikolai participated. It might be somewhat less effective without his participation, but it certainly would not collapse. The church's position within the USSR, then, was much less secure than it had been in 1945, for then the entire operation involving church collaboration with the state could not have been undertaken without the services of the church.

A subtle difference was also present in the new service rendered to the state, one that may have caused considerable discomfort to Nikolai. In the foreign operation begun in 1945, Nikolai had retained a degree of initiative and independence. It was, after all, an operation dealing specifically with churches; unless the state respected Nikolai's judgment, the operation would fail (which is what probably happened). Whatever the ethical compromises and moral dilemmas occasioned by the operation, Nikolai and the church could at least retain that minimum of self-respect derived from their semiautonomous status in the collaboration.

In the PEACE CAMPAIGN Nikolai had lost that independence. He was not a leader in the movement; he had no voice in the planning and direction of the operation. His only choice was to cooperate with it or not. Nikolai was no longer an independent contractor, agreeing to contribute his talents to a joint operation between church and state. His role in the PEACE CAMPAIGN was that of a mere participant echoing the particular order of the day, with little room for independent judgment. His independence, and the church's independence, the last bastion of self-respect, had been removed, and he in effect became little more than a tool of the state's foreign policy.

To be sure, he was no longer subject to some of the ethical questions inherent in the earlier operation. But collaboration with the PEACE CAMPAIGN was not without its ethical problems, and the effect of the change of roles was to exchange the troublesome moral difficulties of the past for new problems that were somewhat more subtle, and hence potentially even more troublesome. A gross evil can eventually be forgotten, or at least dimmed with time. A subtle evil, however, may continue indefinitely, always present, always supplying an undercurrent of uneasiness in all one's activities.

Foremost among the burdensome duties required of Nikolai during the PEACE CAMPAIGN was the necessity to misrepresent the true nature of the Soviet government. To be sure, this was no new requirement, for the megalomania of the Soviet regime had long required ritualistic paeans of praise, and Nikolai had become accustomed to the practice both in his wartime propaganda and in his work immediately following the war. Nevertheless, to continue to lavish praise on the government that had nearly destroyed the church, and that even at its best made church activity restricted and difficult, would represent a continuing annoyance and transgression against honesty.

Who of the impartial and honest people abroad is not aware of the fact that the Russian Orthodox Church, sheltered by the great Stalin Constitution which guarantees freedom of conscience and religious worship, enjoys complete freedom in Her own internal affairs?

• • •

The Russian Orthodox Church will not bless the sword of the new aggressive conquerors, and will not go against the Government, which is the most just government in the country's long and intricate history. In these days, fraught with immense responsibility to future generations, she declares through Her highest representatives with utmost determination for all to hear, that the noble and truly human aims of the Soviet Government, which seek to bring happiness and brotherly love to the working people, are fully supported by the Orthodox Church.[12]

To make such statements as these at a time when conditions within Soviet society were becoming more and more tense, when the increasing severity of the MVD seemed to be building inexorably to a repetition of the Terror of the thirties, seems strange, to say the least. (It should be noted that Nikolai's statement of support for governmental aims is expressed in such a way that he was not necessarily endorsing the specifically anti-Christian aims of the state, such as the eventual abolishment of all religion. Nikolai expresses support for those aims that are in accord with Christian ideals, and does not necessarily include other aims in his statement.)

Similarly, Nikolai's peace activities necessitated a blindness, which must have been self-imposed, to the facts of Soviet acquisition of power. Because of his intimate association with the Soviet conquest of the western Ukraine and Belorussia, he could have had few illusions about the degree of force involved, and, while it may be possible, it does not seem likely that he could have remained ignorant about the large role played by the Red Army and the MVD in the Sovietization of eastern Europe. Nevertheless, he was able to present the PEACE CAMPAIGN in terms that entirely overlooked these bitter realities.

It seems to them that according to fear and mistrust, the only peace possible will be that whereby one of the sides either willingly submits to the other side or else is led to that by force.

· · ·

We Christians believe that the matter of war and peace is in the hands of God, that while there is no war, peace in its usual sense remains in our human hands. This means that we can preserve, strengthen, and prolong it in the measure to which we serve this holy matter.

We Christians are children of freedom and therefore cannot preach a peace dictated by the will of a conqueror, for such a peace signifies physical slavery and spiritual slavery.[13]

At the very least, then, Nikolai's peace activities required a very one-sided vision, which could ignore completely some of the realities he had experienced.

One of the chief requisites for success in propaganda directed at the West is that it be accepted as something other than propaganda. If Nikolai's peace work was to be effective, he would have to be able to claim sincerity and claim that his work was not propaganda at all.

The Russian Orthodox Church cannot have the least hesitation in contributing her efforts to the struggle against the misanthropes. It is necessary to insist on the banning of every form of propaganda that may contribute to the outbreak of war in any country whatsoever. One stems from the other. Thoughts are translated into words, and words into deeds. The word is the direct predecessor of the deed and linked indissolubly with the latter. The word is really a part of the deed, and if the deed is condemned, so, too, must the word be condemned.

Under the present conditions there is absolutely no justification for war. Ungrounded propaganda in favor of war would have no success at all. Hence, propaganda turns to artificial effects—to distortion of facts, to dishonest arguments, to slander and to every form of mendacity.[14]

The problem, of course, was that Soviet propaganda required constant use of precisely those "artificial effects" of which he was here accusing the proponents of war. Nikolai's own speeches conformed so remarkably to the requirements of Soviet propaganda that it was quite apparent that his works were at the very least as culpable in this respect as were such anti-Soviet treatises as he might have been shown.

The difficulties of overcoming this obvious contradiction between the requirements of Soviet policy and those of Christian ideals are apparent in the following passage:

The Church which I here represent stands outside politics because this field of human activity is not characteristic of the spirit and service of the Church. But while it is alien to political calculations and devices, the Church is near to human grief and anxiety; she sees the human motivations by which this or that policy is governed and therefore is able to judge whither and to what end that policy leads. Furthermore, the problems which I would like to touch upon belong as much to the field of the political as they do to the moral order of things.[15]

This is a good argument, reminiscent of the "ratio peccata" developed in similar circumstances by the medieval church in the West. There is a measure of truth in Nikolai's argument. But the problem is that such an argument can only be extended so far before it becomes apparent that the contradiction is much too basic to be smoothed over by such syllogistic simplifications. No amount of verbal facility could long obscure the fact that many of the policies Nikolai was obliged to support in his peace speeches were motivated, not by Christian idealism, but by the hard realities of Soviet state interests.

Despite the inevitable contradictions it involved, Nikolai appears to have had no difficulty in claiming the breadth, comprehensiveness, and objectivity that are so painfully absent from many of his peace utterances. His effectiveness in the Peace Campaign required that he utilize his position in the church to extend the movement's influence, and Nikolai complied fully with this requirement.

The Christian position on which I stand in the decision of all the questions of life guards me from the danger of being slow of understanding or of a onesided point of view. Furthermore, it would be difficult to have a broader and more spiritually independent position, from which one might with greater success defend the interests of all the people without touching their political convictions or regimes.

• • •

As a responsible representative of the Christian world, I, with all decisiveness, affirm that a cause begun under the guise of "defense of Christian civilization" not only has nothing in common with Christianity but is subject to utter condemnation on the part of Christianity.[16]

Nikolai displayed no trace of reticence in using his ecclesiastical position to buttress the credibility of what he had to say. Thus, at a World Peace Congress in Warsaw he said:

I am addressing you here not only as a citizen of my peace-loving Soviet country, I am addressing you also as a bishop of the Russian Orthodox Church and in Her name, with the consciousness of my responsibility to the God I profess, to the Orthodox Church, and to history for every word I utter. . . .[17]

As we have seen, Nikolai's participation in the PEACE CAMPAIGN was essential to the continued functioning of the church within the USSR, and thus, in agreeing to participate at all, he had to accept whatever distasteful necessities might be involved in the contribution he was required to make to the campaign. Even so, one wonders at the apparent equanimity with which his speeches contained statements that were clearly the exact opposite of reality.

The historic mission we are called upon to perform is a noble and lofty one, and our work must be indefatigable and persistent. But ours is not a burdensome task. Among us there is no one who would seek from it personal advantage, profit or privilege. We have no need to resort to dishonest trickery, to wriggle, to evade, to resort to casuistry and sophism, to play with words, to put a double meaning in our conceptions, to present lies as the truth. Our arsenal is quite open; we have no secret weapons or designs. We appeal to the hearts of the common people with words of truth, pointing out that which is clearly apparent to every sane man. Those who oppose us possess gold and a highly perfected and refined apparatus for fabricating lies. Our treasure cannot be transformed into any currency, it can be neither bought nor stolen. Our treasure is the inextinguishable, undying, all-conquering will of humanity to life and peace.[18]

One cannot but wonder whether a degree of inner discouragement might not have accompanied such statements as: "It is necessary to place laws of the Gospel higher than any political consideration whatsoever and by its unity in defense of peace to guarantee the continuation of the work of Christ among peaceful peoples."[19]

In short, Nikolai's peace activities necessitated a continuous dilemma. Candor and honesty could seldom apply. Instead, his statements demanded careful phrasing, presentation of partial truths instead of whole truths, and consideration of a part, but not all, of the situation. In this respect his work contained an inherent tension arising not only from the Christian virtue of truthfulness and the scholarly ideal of objectivity, but even from the basic human preference of truth to falsehood.

While these tensions certainly would represent a considerable ethical problem, it is not likely that it was so great a problem for Nikolai as it might be for a Western churchman. Nikolai was a Russian, and Russia's approach to the virtue of truthfulness differs somewhat from that of the West. Russia had no Renaissance, no Enlightenment. To the extent to which devotion to truth may be a heritage of classical humanism, Russian culture probably is not sensitive to such devotion. The major contact of Soviet society at this time with the ideals of humanism had been filtered through the teachings of Marx and Lenin, and certainly Lenin's humanism knew nothing of that devotion to truth which Western humanism insisted on.[20] Thus to abandon truth for falsehood, while it would present a problem of conscience, might not be so great a moral catastrophe for Nikolai as Westerners might imagine.

Furthermore, Nikolai's concept of truth was probably somewhat different from that of the West. The West, largely because of the centuries of Platonic and Aristotelian influence, sees truth as an ideal to which man, because he is a rational creature, must strive. Truth is something to be sought, to be worked for, to be achieved. This is not so with the Russian church. In the Russian church, truth is not something to be sought, but something to be received. Truth is revealed, not discovered. Truth is accepted on authority; it is validated not by reasoned analysis, but by appeal to the authority of the scriptures, of the fathers, of the Ecumenical Councils, of the church.

Nikolai might be less likely to personalize falsehoods than a Westerner. Orthodox theology traditionally taught submission to the higher powers, including the political, and Nikolai's peace activities were supported by the political authority of his country. Thus Nikolai might be better able to disclaim personal responsibility, at least to a degree, for the ambiguity of his role than would a Western churchman, for he was merely being obedient to the higher authorities, and surely he could not be held entirely responsible for errors and evils committed by that authority. If a given statement of his was false, then that was at least partly the fault of those directing the peace operation.

While such a rationale might partially and temporarily alleviate guilt feelings, it does not seem likely that it could be wholly satisfactory. Dehumanization is the inevitable concomitant of such denial of personal responsibility. Over the long run the cumulative effects of this dehumanization might have created a more critical disruption of the inner life than would a frank admission of guilt, for a moral evil, once accepted, begins to be accepted with the passage of time.

These unpleasant aspects of the work aside, it is possible that Nikolai genuinely believed that the PEACE CAMPAIGN in fact furthered the realization of Christian ideals. Perhaps to some degree it did. With all its deficiencies, the Soviet acceptance of the peace policy was preferable to a nakedly aggressive policy of geographic expansion. Many of the Christian participants in the PEACE CAMPAIGN genuinely believed that it was not an arm of the long-term Soviet aspiration for world domination, but instead was exactly what it claimed to be: a movement whose single goal was the outlawing of war.

Unfortunately, the facts of the matter were that the campaign was a peace movement secondarily; its prime function was to support Soviet policy. Nikolai, because he was so deeply involved in the movement, and because he doubtless was under the supervision of the Soviet state in his activities, could scarcely have cherished many illusions about the matter for long. There was too much evidence to the contrary.

Although the deep sentiment for peace throughout the war-weary world was genuine enough, the PEACE CAMPAIGN was by no means a spontaneous development.[21] As early as 1946 Stalin had publicly spoken of a need to organize this broad sentiment into an anti-Western instrument. Zhdanov had repeated the suggestion shortly thereafter, and the Cominform had followed suit in 1947. The organized PEACE CAMPAIGN was a Soviet creation from the outset, dating from the Wroclaw meeting in 1948. That Nikolai was fully aware that the peace movement originated within the Soviet bloc is apparent from his following statement:

The first demonstration organized by peace supporters was the Wroclaw Congress of Cultural Workers held in April, 1948. Another demonstration was the Women's Congress in Budapest, held in December, 1948. In February, 1949, the Cultural Workers' International Relations Committee and the Bureau of the Women's International Federation took the initiative in convening the World Peace Council.

• • •

Quite naturally, the Soviet Union . . . took a most active part in the Wroclaw and Paris Congresses. Soviet representatives were elected to the Permanent Committee, which continued the work that was initiated by the Congress.[22]

Nikolai could not, then, subscribe to the common misunderstanding that the PEACE CAMPAIGN was apolitical in origin, a creation not of one side or the other in the Cold War, but a movement whose origins were free from political influence. This misconception became increasingly difficult to maintain as the years passed.

In 1950 the campaign's aims were expanded to include militant political action (not excluding violence) designed to frustrate Western activity in Korea.[23] In 1952 one of the leaders of the movement was expelled because of his failure to conform to the Party line against Yugoslavia.[24] The same year, at the Nineteenth Party Congress in Moscow, Stalin bluntly stated that the purposes and functions of the PEACE CAMPAIGN were temporary, and that when the time came for the overthrow of capitalism it would be either transformed into something else or discarded.[25]

The headquarters of the World Peace Council were expelled from Paris in 1950, and the reason the French government gave for its action was that the organization's onesidedness made it harmful to the interests of France. Headquarters were moved to Vienna, and three months after Austrian independence was ratified, in 1955, the World Peace Council was expelled from Austria, again on grounds of its political onesidedness. Thereafter the Secretariat had no headquarters, although the organization's publications were mailed from the International Institute for Peace at the former address of the World Peace Council in Vienna. When the International Institute for Peace was challenged by the Austrian government, it claimed to have no connection whatsoever with the World Peace Council.

Such indices as these of the campaign's subjugation to Soviet policy requirements could be multiplied at length, and Nikolai, who was a member of the Permanent Committee of the World Peace Council,[26] could not possibly have been unaware of them. Thus the basic dilemma of Nikolai's earlier form of collaboration remained during his peace activities. He still was faced by the irreconcilability of Christian ideals with the aspirations of Soviet foreign policy.

There were numerous specific falsehoods that Nikolai had to embrace in the course of his peace activities, of course, but these specifics almost seem piquant when compared with the fundamental ethical problems we have been reviewing. In 1954, for example, long after the Soviet state had announced that the Western monopoly of nuclear fusion weapons was ended, Nikolai said the following in one of his speeches:

When the hydrogen bomb was exploded on Bikini and the fatal consequences of this explosion were marked, all the peoples of our planet were indignant in spirit, but they did not fall into despair. The experiment with the hydrogen bomb evoked not fear but protest. . . .

If, before the explosion of the hydrogen bomb, many among the people had already nourished several illusions relating to its moral consequences on intended antagonists, in view of the terrible and unforeseen consequences of this explosion, the people of all nations, religions and persuasions understood the danger to which all mankind and all its culture is subjected.

It can be said that the explosion of the hydrogen bomb, which evoked an explosion of indignation in the moral sphere, broke down many partitions and divisions between people. The human world became profoundly disturbed. To this time it is agitated as an ocean before the storms, and powerful waves of protests rush about the face of the whole earth requiring the immediate prohibition of atomic and hydrogen weapons for which the Russian Orthodox Church has loudly been raising its voice during all the recent years.[27]

It is unthinkable that Nikolai was unaware of the one-sidedness of ignoring the Soviet government's share in the guilt of hydrogen weapons development.

In another instance Nikolai tried to give a direct answer to the Western charge that Soviet rule was tyrannical. Apparently without difficulty, he temporarily ignored the darker side of the experiences of his entire life as a churchman under Soviet rule and of his work in the western Ukraine:

They fear the thought that to renounce war with the East means to capitulate to "tyranny."

But where is this "tyranny," when it is precisely the East which raises the issue of prohibition of atomic weapons and general disarmament. Nor are the marks of "tyranny" evident in those efforts of the East which are expressed to them, that peace be attained in Korea, that peace treaties be concluded with Germany and Austria and agreement be reached with the West on peaceful coexistence.

On the contrary, from these evident facts there follows only one conclusion about the preparedness of the East to compete with the West in ameliorating the conditions of life of the peoples. And such a possibility should be especially welcome to Christians in the sense of the defence of peace, of ameliorating the social conditions of life and the installation of Christian beginnings in [those conditions].[28]

It was in the propaganda surrounding the Korean War that Nikolai's peace activities are best summarized. Here he was able to give full expression to his talents for unrestrained invective. In his Korean War speeches he gave:

. . . warning to the gang of maniacs, to the moral degenerates, to the infuriated parasites, to the infanticides in tail-coats and general's uniforms, to the fiends and butchers of the human race, who are endeavoring to put a torch to the splendid home of mankind.[29]

Once again he found his previous familiarity with war-time propaganda applicable. His acquaintance with German atrocities during his service with the War Crimes Commission was useful also. And while it would have been exceedingly difficult to believe that only the West was guilty of aggression, the controlled press in the USSR would provide a basis for claiming ignorance of conflicting evidence.

The problem with such a claim, however, is its credibility. One of the almost universal concomitants of a controlled press is a high degree of skepticism among its readers. The populace becomes decreasingly open to persuasion by a controlled press, and learns either to disregard completely what is said in it or to practice the skill of "reading between the lines," particularly when matters are expressed in grandiose, exaggerated terms. If this skepticism insulates rank-and-file citizens from the controlled press, could a person of such intelligence, training, and experience as Nikolai credibly claim on these grounds complete ignorance of the possibility of conflicting evidence?

Whatever the case, Nikolai seemed able to present an exceedingly biased picture of the Korean conflict, as in the following extract:

It is well known how on June 25, 1950, the hordes of America's Korean puppet, Li Seung Man, basely attacked the Korean People's Democratic Republic on the orders of their American masters. The careful preparations for this vile action are also well known.

• • •

It is well known what methods the United States of America employed, and is employing, to force its resolutions through the United Nations.

It is well known with what demagogic howls the American propagandists are endeavouring to conceal the bestial fangs of imperialism that are bared to the whole world.

• • •

Yet another circumstance of the Korean events is well known, and it is to this circumstance that I wish to draw your attention. I have in mind the methods the American aggressors are using to conduct the war in Korea.

When we turn to the official declarations made by statesmen of the Korean People's Democratic Republic; when we listen to the evidence of war correspondents, some of whom are not particularly progressive in their views; when we hear what is related by people who miraculously survived the retreat of the occupying troops, or by those who succeeded in fleeing from the accursed regions of the "new American order"—when we do this we experience feelings that no document can convey, we sense the abyss of boundless, inconsolable grief into which these modern American monsters have hurled a noble people with an ancient culture.

We see, then, that the spirit and the flesh of fascism have not disappeared, that there are some who are continuing the delirious dreams of the fanatic Hitler and are attempting to make them come true.

The followers have nothing to learn from their teachers.

No sooner had they begun their criminal aggression than the American neo-fascists began the planned, cannibalistic extermination of the "inferior" Korean race.

What do we see?

Brazen flouting not only of the norms of international law but of all standards of human morality. Executions without trial or investigation, held in secret and in public. Terrible mutilation of victims: they cut off ears, noses and breasts, gouge out eyes, break arms and legs, crucify patriots, bury women and infants alive, and so on. Revival of the customs of savages—they scalp Korean patriots for "souvenirs."

To exterminate the population the American criminals first of all fiendishly slaughtered political prisoners (from 200,000 to 400,000 people), forcing them to dig their own graves beforehand; the bodies of the patriots who were hanged or shot or who died from typhus were flung into a ravine, and the cliff blown up to cover the traces of the crime. The barbaric bombing of peaceful towns and villages has been carried out solely for the purpose of annihilating the civilian population.

In the American army investigating commissions we see a revival of the Himmler "technique," inhuman torture of Korean patriots: they hang them up by the hands tied behind the back, a torture which is barefacedly called "the airplane"; they manacle them with handcuffs behind the back for two to three months; they torture them by electricity, including an electric bed where death is brought on by means of a powerful electric current; they use a wet leather jacket, which on drying crushes the chest of the victim; they place men suffering from infectious diseases in overcrowded cells.

These civilized savages arrange shooting competitions with live targets, binding peasants to posts with barbed wire and firing at targets fixed over the hearts of each man. Resurrecting the customs of the fascist hoodlums, the Yankee hoodlums photographed such scenes for their family albums and sent them home to their wives and sweethearts.

These representatives of the "superior" race have been and are committing mass rape of Korean women and girls, herding them from surrounding villages, making them drunk on gin and raping them. Not stopping at such outrage, in some places they drove the unfortunates into tunnels which they blew up after machine-gunning the victims.

On the roads of Korea it is a common sight to see the yet warm corpse of a mother with a nursing child crying at her breast. Cases have been known when children born in prison were trampled underfoot by soldiers' boots before the eyes of their mothers, after which the mothers too were murdered.

When retreating, this "flower of culture" destroyed or drove along with them every living thing from the districts left behind.

When advancing, their rage likewise descended first and foremost on peaceful citizens.

Thus, at the landing on September 15 in the Bay of Inchon every living thing in the district was exterminated by insensate barrages day and night. During the offensive against Seoul in September 1950 the same tactics of general extermination were employed.

In September 1950 the French journalist Charles Favrel visited a death camp situated in the "valley of horror" in South Korea. In this camp over 300,000 Koreans are doomed to death. At that time there were ten such camps, each surrounded by barbed wire charged with strong electric current. The people live on the bare earth, they have neither clothes nor shoes. They are not fed; they eat grass and the bark of trees and bushes. Under the pretext of affording them medical aid American scientists and doctors experiment on the prisoners with the latest vaccines and chemical preparations. Every night executions take place in the ravines surrounding the camp. First on the list for destruction are the intelligentsia of Korea: doctors, teachers, engineers, technicians, agromonists.

• • •

When retreating in January 1951 the occupying troops forcibly drove into South Korea more than two million peaceful citizens, thousands of whom died on the way in the roadside ditches from cold and starvation and from the bullets of the aggressors.

Hunger and epidemics awaited those of the peaceful civilians of North Korea who survived and were cast into camps in the South. Even the notorious U.N. Commission on Korea in its letter to the United Nations of February 1, 1951, notes that 3,628,000 Koreans have been left homeless and destitute.

Especially do the occupants vent their fury on the children of Korea. Wherever they have set foot—in the provinces of South Pyongyang, North Hamgen, South Hamgen, Kengi, Kanwong—the American bandits have slaughtered children.

And one cannot but recall that the ideological leaders of the gruesome events in Korea consider themselves Christians, and not merely Christians, but even leaders of Christian organizations! They know the Bible and quite frequently announce this fact for all to hear!

The mind can give no explanation to this nightmare, and the heart does not cease to contract with a feeling of holy horror at the cannibals. The conscience of all common people cries out against the atrocities of the American aggressors!

Across the whole of the world spread waves of protest and indignation against the American aggression in Korea and the atrocities perpetrated by the occupants; against the attempts to unleash another world war by means of blocs and pacts and the remilitarization of Germany and Japan; against the use of the U.N. by the United States of America as a weapon of aggression. This indignation against the crazed and insensate rulers who are dragging the nations into an abyss rings out in numberless petitions sent to parliaments and governments. It can be heard in the utterances of women and young people in all countries of the world. Crowds of people thousands strong assembling on city squares in Europe voice their protest and indignation, demanding that these cosmopolitan racketeers from across the ocean and world colonizers in dress-suits and generals' uniforms go back where they came from.

We who are fighting for world peace have a great and sacred responsibility to future generations. Tirelessly and persistently we must multiply our ranks, explain to the duped, to the doubters, to the indifferent, to the escapists all the dire danger of their position, open their eyes to the true state of affairs in the world, instill hope and confidence in their hearts.[30]

By the time of the Korean War the world was becoming accustomed to the excesses of the peace propagandists, and such speeches as this seldom were taken very seriously. Regardless of one's political position, it would be difficult to become much exercised over such a witless display of propaganda in a matter of such seriousness and importance. Aside from the questionable ethics of such extremism, the pointlessness of such undisciplined and tasteless use of invective —bordering on stupidity if not complete silliness—seems incompatible with the finesse and tact that were Nikolai's accustomed habit. Perhaps the insult to intelligence of Soviet propaganda requirements would be as distasteful a burden as the ethical contradictions were.

In any case, memory is short, and the impact of such tirades—as, indeed, of nearly all of Nikolai's peace utterances —is quickly forgotten. There were two areas, however, not so quickly forgotten, and that quite possibly (in one case, definitely) had an influence on Nikolai's life thereafter.

One of these areas had to do with the relations of Russian Orthodoxy with Western Christianity. During the heyday of the PEACE CAMPAIGN, Nikolai's attitude toward Western Christianity was determined by the simple criterion of whether or not such Christians participated in the campaign.

For example, in a section of a 1952 speech in Moscow directed specifically to Christians of the West, he said:

All religious people without exception must support the Appeal of the Bureau of the World Peace Council [condemning the use of bacteriological warfare in Korea and elsewhere]. . . .

Since there are no worshippers of evil and falsehood among us, we cannot have different opinions regarding our common need of peace, nor can there be any dispute among us concerning the means of achieving it.[31]

Nikolai clearly implies that anyone holding a different view (specifically, in this case, on the germ warfare issue) is a worshiper of evil and falsehood.

The facts of the matter were that only those churches within the Soviet empire gave any considerable support to the PEACE CAMPAIGN, particularly after it had become apparent that it was not politically free in many of its positions. Among the PEACE CAMPAIGN luminaries, Protestant clergymen from the West were represented only by a scattered few individuals. Catholics from the West were represented not at all. Thus Nikolai's division of Christians into peaceful and aggressive camps was almost a verbatim repetition of the fiction promulgated at the council of 1948, that world Christianity consisted of the peace-loving, democratic Orthodox and the aggressive, capitalistic Protestants and Catholics.

Many Christians of the West still take an ambiguous position: although they speak of their adherence to the idea of international peace, they continue to lean on the "policy of force."

Sometimes one can think that in this policy it is not war itself which attracts them, nor even the conviction that it can serve as a path to righteousness, but [they are influenced by] a moment of fear of an imagined adversary and of bringing him to submission. The danger of this point of view is as great as its naïveté.

Other Christians are inclined to consider aggressive war as a "lesser evil," forgetting that the evil of contemporary war and its finality surpass everything which can be placed by them in its justification.

There are also Christians for whom war, according to their opinion, is the last refuge. But this view on war testifies not of a Christian attitude, but of a feeling of hostility and hate.[32]

Nikolai's expressed attitude toward Western Christianity was even more narrowly defined than the criterion of participation in the PEACE CAMPAIGN. Any Christian who was willing to countenance use of force for any reason was unacceptable, and the logic of Nikolai's position would render anything short of total pacifism reprehensible to Christianity. Immediately after the outbreak of the Korean War, Nikolai had specifically disallowed even defensive warfare on the part of the West.

When the "defenders" of civilization, displaying their solicitude for reducing the "surplus" population in other than the western countries, discuss in business-like fashion the comparative merits of atomic and bacteriological weapons—this, at any rate, faithfully reflects their schemes. When these very same men try to justify their military measures by "defense" considerations, the masking of their aggressive intentions is wholly transparent. But when they try to base their misanthropic policy on the high authority of the Christian religion, they are attempting to commit a colossal fraud.

The danger of this fraud is that in their fight against the People's Democracies and Communism the imperialists proclaim themselves defenders of Christianity. In this they are abetted by certain ecclesiastical leaders of western creeds who are connected with them by interests that are in no way spiritual. We all know the rôle of the Vatican—that sworn enemy of the peoples who are defending peace; this rôle calls for our condemnation; it cannot fail to evoke a shudder in every honest heart.[33]

The Vatican was the *bête noire* of Nikolai's peace propaganda. Soviet foreign policy had been carrying on campaigns of unremitting bitterness against the Vatican since the twenties, and hostility to the Catholic church was by now a Soviet tradition.[34] Certainly since World War II, when Russian Orthodoxy joined the state's propaganda campaign against the Vatican, Nikolai had come to be able to denounce Catholicism simply from habit. Nikolai's identification with the state's attack against the Roman church would certainly militate against any possibility of lessening the hostility, as witness the following section from his peace propaganda:

The Russian Orthodox Church, while having due regard for the mass of believers of the Roman Catholic Church, cannot shut Her eyes to the doings of the group which has usurped the authority and the rights of the Church and which is inspiring, spiritually and practically, the currently raging war hysteria. Never once in the course of the Second World War did the Papal Throne raise its voice in protest against the butchers of humanity, or in defense of the millions slaughtered, tortured, condemned to rot in jail, hanged, shot or asphyxiated in the terrible "murder vans." Its voice was raised only once—when the assassins were being tried. It was raised in defense of the assassins. Now the head of the Roman Catholic Church, blinded by an old malice toward the Orthodox, especially toward the Slavs, and to the highest degrees toward the Russian Soviet people—now that long-time sworn enemy of the Soviet Union has openly joined the sinister camp of incendiaries of a new war. All the world knows that he is an agent of American imperialism.

We consider it a blasphemous trampling of the most fundamental principles of Christianity when we see how the Christian religion, with the collusion of its high Catholic representatives, is being unscrupulously used in the class interests of the capitalist rulers of Europe and America, to help oppress and exploit the working masses and to pave the way for another bloody shambles.

The Pope revealed his antichristian face in all its spiritual ugliness by his recent decree excommunicating Communists and those who sympathize with the latter, the decree which fundamentally contradicts the basic principles of the Christian Gospel and which came into being in consequence of the beastly malice harboured by the head of the Roman Catholic Church.[35]

Some of the Catholic newspapers, no doubt inspired from above, are continuing to assert that the Church in the Soviet Union is "not free," is "held in captivity," is "enslaved," is subordinated to the Soviet Government and administered by the latter. One gets to wondering whether these allegations of yesterday's, and possibly of tomorrow's, accomplices in international crime contain more bigotry or more shortsighted reckoning on the ignorance of the masses.[36]

At the time, these statements of hostility toward Western Christianity were directly in line with Soviet foreign policy. But should state interests ever change in the direction of seeking broader contact with Western Christianity,[37] the fear that these statements might be remembered could seriously reduce Nikolai's effectiveness as the chief representative of Russian Orthodoxy in foreign affairs.

The issue that was to have the greatest effect on Nikolai's subsequent life was that of germ warfare. In February 1952 Soviet propaganda began a massive campaign charging the United States with the use of bacteriological weapons in Korea.[38] The PEACE CAMPAIGN followed suit, and for the next year this was one of its primary emphases. Naturally,

Nikolai took part in this propaganda. The sudden hue and cry over germ warfare may have come as something of a surprise to him, however, for he had all along been accustomed to including such a charge in his list of accusations in the Korean conflict. In September 1950 he had written an article that stated:

They are manufacturing bacteriological weapons, which already demonstrated their action in Eastern China. [The footnote reads, "The town of Chinhua, which in 1940 was in the center of the East-China front, was subjected to bacteriological bombardment which resulted in an epidemic of plague destroying almost the entire population."] Plague, cholera, typhus and other deadly germs are bred in laboratories; poisonous substances are concocted for the mass destruction of people, animals and wheat crops over huge areas.[39]

He returned to the subject in passing a month later by denouncing a statement attributed to an American professor: "I would approve bacteriological warfare, gas, atomic and hydrogen bombs and intercontinental rockets."[40]

Nikolai had always been willing to include germ warfare in the list of heinous crimes of the West, but he never had paid a great deal of attention to that particular charge, using it only as one among many. Even after Soviet propaganda had chosen that specific issue for a major campaign, Nikolai, while he cooperated with the campaign, did not seem especially enthusiastic or excited about it.

However much the instigators of warfare by plague, cholera, and typhus may try to cover the tracks of their crimes, they are sternly convicted by the facts which have been established and verified by authoritative international commissions, as we heard just today from the mouths of participants of these commissions themselves. Attempts to contradict these crimes show that the criminals are terrified by the indignation of the peoples and are afraid of exposure. Whether this is indicative of fear of responsibility or of a desire to preserve the remainders of prestige, in any case we are dealing with a bloody and completely amoral enemy. Therefore it is necessary to do everything possible in order to render him harmless.

In warning of new crimes, it is necessary to appeal first of all to the American people, before whom stands the question of honor and self-respect, as was stated in the appeal of the Bureau of the World Peace Council. For the Christian Americans this signifies moral responsibility for the actions of their government: in the name of the high principles of the Christian religion they should demand that it stop the bacteriological warfare and abide by the Geneva Convention of 1925. In the achievement of both goals, the American Christians should see the justification of their faith, as in the punishment of the criminals of bacteriological warfare the American people will see the salvation of their honor and self-respect.[41]

Nikolai returned to the subject a few times during the course of 1952, but he never appears to have made a great issue of it, although in one of his speeches he mentioned the issue in passing, "It is necessary daily to require the outlawing of atomic and bacteriological weapons and the cessation of armed activity in Korea, Vietnam, and Malaya."[42] Even at the Conference of All the Churches and Religious Societies in the USSR, held May 9–12, 1952, at the height of the bacteriological campaign, he was content merely to mention that the Orthodox church had protested that crime in the press a few weeks earlier.

The matter of consolidating peace requires immediate prohibition of atomic, chemical, bacteriological, and all other arms of mass destruction of people, in order to dispel fear and mutual distrust among people, which raise obstacles to the agreement of the sides.

All believers as one should unite themselves to the call of the

Bureau of the World Peace Council against bacteriological arms, that great shame of our days.

With special hope we turn to the millions of believing Americans. Since you constitute the huge majority of the population of the United States of America, you have every possibility to compel your government to observe the generally accepted norms of conduct and to adhere to the international Convention of June 17, 1925, which prohibits the use of poisonous gases and bacteriological means in war.[43]

It should not be inferred from this comparatively mild attitude that Nikolai was unwilling to join in the campaign. He did cooperate fully but, in comparison with some of his other utterances, even the following statement does not seem particularly enthusiastic:

Wildly and shamelessly violating the elementary norms of international law and the principles of humanity, the American aggressors, as we have learned from the governments of the Korean People's Democratic Republic and People's China, have taken an utterly inhuman step by beginning, in Korea and Northeast China, bacteriological warfare—a form of warfare outlawed by international convention. They are dropping the germs of plague, cholera and typhus from airplanes on the civilian population of Korea and on the positions of the valiant Korean People's Army and the Chinese volunteers.[44]

Nikolai cooperated in the germ warfare campaign, but he just did not seem to care very much about it. Therefore there is a great deal of irony in the fact that it was precisely this issue that was to challenge him four years later, and the resurrection of this (to Nikolai) minor issue was to inaugurate a dramatic change in his life.

VII

The Pastor: Death and Life Beyond

NIKOLAI'S SERMONS REGULARLY return to the subject of death and the life beyond, so regularly, in fact, that these subjects represent a sizable portion of the sermons' contents. This is by no means unusual, for concentration on the future life has been one of the identifying characteristics of Russian Orthodoxy throughout the Soviet period.

One of the reasons for this emphasis is the circumscribed position in which the church finds itself in Soviet life. Freedom of religion is guaranteed to all citizens by Soviet law, but it is a peculiar sort of freedom. According to Article 124 of the 1936 Constitution of the USSR (the "Stalin Constitution"), "In order to guarantee freedom of conscience, all citizens are guaranteed freedom of religious worship and of antireligious propaganda." Thus the only legally permissible activities of the church are those involving worship.

But the restriction is even more stringent than it might seem. The Russian word translated "worship" means, more properly, "cultus" or "liturgy." The meaning of the law is that only the normal worship services of the church are allowed; any other activities, even though they might constitute worship in one form or another, are illegal. Thus it is against the law for the church to engage in many of the activities that other societies take for granted as essential to religious liberty. Activities other than the worship services, such as men's, women's, or youth groups, are illegal. Charitable activities are prohibited. Public or social welfare programs are of course unthinkable, as are programs of evangelistic outreach or community service. Recreational activities (church dinners or picnics, church sports) are not possible. All educational activities for children, such as Sunday schools, are against the law.[1]

Because of these limitations on its activities, the church is forced to confine its interests to the purely religious activity permitted by law. The church is unable to engage in non-worship activities; hence it is not unnatural that matters of eternity occupy a large share of its concern.

In addition to the legal limitations on its interests, the church is also restricted by extralegal limitations. The state exercises exceedingly close supervision over the activities of the churches. In particular, sermons delivered during worship services are subject to strict censorship. In some cases, the Secret Police exercise prior censorship directly by recruiting the priest to their service (sometimes through threat or blackmail). More often, sermons are submitted in advance to the priest's secretary, who is usually in direct contact with the Secret Police. Censorship of the sermon during its delivery is exercised by stationing at least one (and usually several) informers in the congregation, whose duty is to take notes on what transpires. (Sermons that are later published, are subject to the additional censorship inherent in a controlled press.)

Thus Russian Orthodox sermons must avoid topics likely

to be unacceptable to the state. Social issues, such as injustice or a low level of public morality, never appear in the sermons. Political issues are also wholly absent, except for a very few specifically permissible subjects such as the peace movement. Even ethical subjects must be treated with great caution, for too sweeping a treatment of many common errors could reflect unflatteringly on the government. The result is that ethical matters, when they are treated at all, are treated devotionally rather than socially.[2]

The only truly safe subjects for sermons in the USSR are those that deal with purely theological matters. Given the extreme restriction of its permissible interests, the Orthodox church's chief duty is to prepare its people for the life beyond the grave[3]; counseling them publicly on their conduct in this life, because it risks incurring the displeasure of the state, takes a relatively minor position. One of the chief interests of the church is the ultimate issue of salvation and damnation, of death and the Judgment, of eternal bliss and eternal misery.

It is ironic that the pressure of the Communist regime has so directly reinforced Orthodoxy's natural tendency toward other-worldliness. According to communist dogma, Christianity (and all religion) is a remnant of capitalist exploitation. Its chief function is to pacify the oppressed workers by inducing them to endure present misery in the hope of some mythical future reward. The legal restrictions on religion in the USSR have done much to guarantee that the church will continue to perform a similar function in Soviet society, offering the hope of future justice to many who may have felt themselves exploited by the harsh realities of Soviet rule.

The ultimate irony is that by forcing the church to concentrate on other-worldliness, the Communist state forces it to emphasize the one area in which communist ideology is least able to compete. The totalitarian efficiency of Soviet rule has demonstrated an ability to answer questions of social justice, such as starvation and unemployment (although it should be noted that Soviet solutions to these injustices have not always conformed in every particular to Christian concepts of justice). With its control over the press, the state has also been able to claim great strides in eradicating crime and in rehabilitating criminals. If the church had been able to concern itself with social issues, it would have faced a formidable competitor in the state, and there is every reason to believe that the efficiency of the state might have won the competition by showing that the Communist government was better equipped to deal with such issues than was the Christian church.

But communism has had no such demonstrable success in dealing with man's ultimate questions, the questions that arise from the crises of life and from the deep longing of man to be free, to be just, to be morally clean and at peace with himself. Christianity can provide satisfaction for these yearnings of man, whereas communist morality,[4] because it is all but limited to sociological arguments, has been woefully unsatisfactory to the rank and file of its citizens. In time of crisis, such as war or catastrophe, it has been the church, not the Party, to which the people repaired. At the crucial events in life—birth, marriage, death—the state has never succeeded in competing with Christian rituals and celebrations.

It is particularly in the crisis of death that communism has been absolutely powerless. The only consolation Soviet Marxism provides is the rather fatuous assertion of the immortality of society, which lives on after the death of any particular unit of society.[5] Such an answer is scant solace for those who have been bereaved or who are facing the problem of their own death. Christian answers—personal immortality and eternal communion with God—have a power with which the Communist Party of the Soviet Union cannot compete.

Thus it is understandable that death and the future life occupied a large place in Nikolai's sermons. Very often his sermons give an impression of partial alienation from this life. "We all here on earth are strangers and travellers," he would declare, "our native country is not here. . . . Our eternal fatherland is there, in heaven."[6]

On graveside markers in our cemeteries we often read other sacred words: "Blessed are the dead who die in the Lord." (Rev. 14:13) These words tell us of those who on their way to heaven have already experienced the happiness of life with God in the Spirit and have walked with Him into the Eternal World. This constitutes the goal of life for each of us: to live with the Lord and to die with Him. The fruit of such a life will also be blessed: eternal fellowship with God and eternal presence in that World where there is neither sorrow nor crying nor sighing.[7]

Earthly life is seen in the colors of the future life of blessedness. The aura of the supernatural penetrates backward in time through the barrier of death, so that, ideally, life before death is lived in terms of life after death.

And now, when the curtain on the life beyond is lifted before man, when man knows that endless eternity stretches before him, what an elevated, high-principled meaning is revealed in his earthly life, its goal, its sense; what a priceless happiness it has become for man. Earthly life is a step to life eternal, a path of preparation of the self for life which knows no end. The light of the word of God, revealing to us the mystery of death, also enlightens us to the mysteries of those joys which await us in the future city of the Heavenly Jerusalem, not made with hands, revealed to us in the Divine Revelation, sparkling with its eternal, incorruptible beauties and rewarding all its future inhabitants with absolutely incomparable eternal spiritual delights! To live such as to be worthy of these joys—this is the holy and joyous task of earthly life. And each of our souls knows now that this happiness of eternal life, happiness of eternal fellowship with its spiritually Sweet Lord will not only be a fruit on completion of an earthly life worthy of it, but it already has a beginning here, in the earthly life of each of us, and is the property of each heart which lives in God and with God as the source of this happiness.[8]

This emphasis on the transcendent, rather than the natural, aspect of life is another common element in Russian Christianity. Russia never experienced anything like the Western Liberal movement in its religious life. Biblical criticism never penetrated into Russia, and Scripture is still considered as an oracular revelation. This is as true of Russian Orthodoxy as it is of the most benighted and fanatical sects on the fringes of Russian Protestantism.[9] It is true even of many nonbelievers. One of the surprising incongruities of Soviet atheism is the often-repeated attempt to discredit the Bible by demonstrating that the miracles had scientific bases, rather than merely discounting the miraculous events altogether, as Western secular man is accustomed to do.[10]

Nor did any of the theologies of modern Western Christianity have any great impact on Russian Orthodoxy. Theology, for the Orthodox, begins with the Scriptures and ends with St. John Chrysostom.[11] (The Marxists did only a little better; their familiarity with modern theology does not include much after Spinoza.[12]) The many Western attempts to work out a theology less dependent on an unexamined supernaturalism and more compatible with modern thought were all but unheard of in Nikolai's church.

It should not seem strange, then, that Nikolai's sermons are more inclined to the supernatural than are many Western sermons. Western sermons often display a great appreciation of the practical, public, and social requirements of the faith. Not so with Russian Orthodoxy; the profoundly supernatural elements of the Christian faith—death and eternal life— lie much closer to the heart of the Orthodox believer.

Even were the traditions of Orthodoxy less inclined toward the areas of mystery in life, Nikolai would have had to spend some time considering the inevitable events that await each man, whether he wished to or not. Russian Orthodoxy during all these years of Nikolai's leadership was engaged in a quiet, unpublicized struggle with a formidable competitor for the affections of the Orthodox people: the underground Orthodox movement.[13] Underground Orthodoxy had existed from the twenties but grew especially powerful in the decade following World War II. According to Soviet scholars, the postwar underground movement consisted of two separate branches: a highly organized clandestine church, the True Orthodox Church, and a less organized, less militant branch, the True Orthodox Christians. This movement, which rejected the legalized patriarchal church because of its accommodation with the atheistic regime (although in many cases underground groups probably appeared simply because there was no church whatsoever in which the people could worship), was a truly formidable competitor. The True Orthodox Christians were more numerous in some regions than all other non-Orthodox religious groups combined during the late forties and early fifties.[14] The seriousness of this competition was reflected in the many oblique references to nonpatriarchal Orthodoxy in the *Journal of the Moscow Patriarchate* during this period.[15]

The chief emphasis of underground Orthodoxy's theology

(insofar as underground Orthodoxy had a theology) was apocalypticism. The Soviet state was the Antichrist, and the patriarchal church was his servant. Two apocalyptic works composed in the twenties, along with the biblical books *Daniel* and *Revelation,* enjoyed great popularity in underground Orthodoxy and were widely disseminated in manuscript form. The end of the world, sometimes identified with World War III, was expected momentarily.

Apocalypticism is by no means a strange phenomenon among people so thoroughly alienated from society. The lives of the illegal Orthodox Christians were insecure in the extreme. They were miserably poor and, because they were largely cut off from the economic life of society, hunger was never far away. Their days were spent in fear, and their nights in dread of the knock of the Secret Police on their doors. Small wonder that apocalypticism was so attractive to them.

But all Christians in Soviet society were in a similar position during the decade following the war. Weapons of mass destruction, the imminence of new war (which, according to the Soviet press, would be unleashed by the West momentarily), and the fresh memories of the horrors of World War II combined to make the lives of all Soviet citizens insecure to a degree. The great mass of the population was also poor, due to the emphasis on heavy industry and the military to the complete neglect of consumer needs, and, although hunger may have been an imminent prospect for only a minority, very few Soviet citizens could feel economically secure during these years. And with the increasing totalitarianism of Stalin's last years, all Soviet citizens were subject to possible investigation by the MVD.

Thus all citizens participated to some degree in the disabilities with which the underground Orthodox had to live.

In particular, the Christians of legal Orthodoxy shared the same alienation from society because of communism's deep hostility to religion. If the exciting prospects of an imminent return of Christ, of sudden and final punishment of the wicked, and of the impending appearance of a truly just and happy order were attractive to the fugitives in the underground church, apocalypticism would also offer a tempting attraction to the members of the legal church.

Nikolai had to find some way to counteract the appeal of apocalypticism, and his frequent discourses on death and immortality served this purpose. Death, after all, is the personal *eschaton,* the end of the world so far as the individual is concerned, and an appreciation of the imminence of death, judgment, and entrance into the heavenly kingdom can serve the same purpose for an individual that apocalypticism can serve for a group. The topic of death, in Nikolai's sermons, was in part an individualized form of apocalypticism.

The day of the Divine Judgment, called the Terrible Judgment, will come. From the words of Christ we know that we will stand at this Judgment not only in our immortal soul. Before that, by the power of God, at the sound of the Archangel's trumpet the dead will rise. Wherever the bodies of people may be—whether in the earth or at the bottom of seas and oceans—both land and water will give up their dead. The risen bodies, by the teaching of our faith, will arise sanctified, renovated, freed from all our present weaknesses and needs, will rise so that they may be joined to the eternal soul of each of us. At the Terrible Judgment of God each of us will have to give answer for everything that was done in our earthly life.

• • •

Each of us prepares himself to participate. Both future torment and future joy for each of us will be the fruit of that life which each of us lives and with which each of us dies. That "reward" for the poor in spirit, for the meek, for the merciful about which the Lord speaks in His Beatitudes will not be any sort of external reward to a person for his feats but will be a continuation and deepening of that happiness to live with God and to fulfill His Holy Will which the true servant of God already bears in his earthly life.

•   •   •

Death is not. But one must prepare for death for his whole life because death is the door to eternity.[16]

There was another function of such passages in Nikolai's sermons that was far deeper, far more fundamental, and far more indicative of the peculiar, personal approach to the Orthodox church reflected in those sermons. Just as the pietistic, devotional approach to Christianity may have provided a sort of haven from the intolerable reality of life in an evil world, so the consideration of death and the beyond may have served a similar function.

Soviet life during the Stalin era was stern, hard, and unyielding. It offered no quarter for the weak or tired. Russia was given no breathing spell after the war, no time to lick its wounds. The harsh tempo of rebuilding, of industrializing, of rearming was resumed without pause after the war, and for many years thereafter life continued to be difficult and demanding.

But the harshness of Soviet life had a deeper cause than this. In part, unrelenting pressure seems to be a legacy of communism itself. The mood of communism is basically idealistic.[17] All of its leaders, from Marx to Stalin's successors, embraced the peculiar apocalyptic of communist dogma, a future age of utopian perfection to be ushered in by the cataclysmic destruction of capitalism. The chief and only motivation of communism (ignoring, for a moment, the thirst for personal aggrandizement of some of its leaders, which really should have no place in communism) is an idealistic commitment to reform, to overcome injustice and exploitation, to create for the people a society in which all evil will at last have disappeared. Communists are idealists and reformers.

And nobody is quite so intolerant and unpitying as the person who is totally committed to idealistic reform. Long before the arrival of communism in Russia, Dostoyevsky, in whom the spirit of Russian Orthodoxy was most vividly expressed, had foreseen the cruelty and terror that unrestrained reforming idealism would unleash.[18] All of the horrors of Soviet history were committed in the name of communism's idealism. There was little place in Stalin's Russia for tolerance, for forgiveness, for pity.

It was the Russian Orthodox Church that provided this sorely needed part of life. Here was forgiveness for sin and shortcoming, here was acceptance without regard to how successful one's public life might be. Here was a place for softness and beauty, where one could find rest from the strident, energetic *fortissimo* of Soviet propaganda and music and art, where the muscularity of "Soviet realism" in art and public statuary was replaced by the fragile, mysterious tranquility of the icon. One needed only to contemplate the icons of the church to find that indulgence and human pity which were so painfully absent from the Soviet climate.

Perhaps the most bitter climax of the harshness of communism is to be found in the problem of death. The bland assurance that society is immortal even if society's units are not may satisfy a devoted optimist, but for most people that answer to the problem of personal death is a climax of cruelty, of inhumanity, of pitilessness. It is precisely in Nikolai's sermons that an alternative is to be found, for the church does care, does answer:

The hour of death will come for each of us and our Church
will guide our immortal soul onto the path of eternal life by her
last words of parting and blessings. Our corpse will be brought
hither into the holy temple and the funereal sobbing of our
bearers will mingle with the graveside prayers of the holy
Church for the peace of our sinful soul in the Heavenly Kingdom. She will never forget us, her children: and then, when we
will not be here with you, when on earth there will not be even
those who, after our death, according to their love toward us
still might give a memorial with a reminder for the peace of
our souls—the prayers of the Holy Church for us will never
become silent. On the [festival] Sabbaths of Parents the Holy
Church will remember to the end of the age all the grand-
fathers, fathers, and brothers who have died in the Orthodox
faith.[19]

The difficult part of Nikolai's approach to the reality of
death was that it made requirements on the life of the person. If Nikolai's approach were really to be comforting,
then life must be lived in conformity to the faith.

Such an end [to life], Christian and unshameful, cannot be
by chance, is not the result only of our desire—be it even
fervent—alone. We do not see fruit ripened all at once on a
tree. In the spring it begins, in summer it fills out and ripens,
and in the autumn we pick it. And an unshameful Christian life
should precede an unshameful Christian death.[20]

To accept Nikolai's answer would raise great tension if a
person's conscience were troubled by knowledge of evil in
his own life. If a man knew that he had transgressed the
ethical demands of Christianity, if he knew that his life was
embracing moral evil, then to accept such a doctrine could
not but create an inner dilemma, a tension within, which
really could not be resolved so long as those morally unacceptable actions were continued. The sword cut both ways:

Nikolai's sermons, when they dealt with death and the future life, gave a promise of bliss, but they also gave assurance of judgment for those whose lives fell short of the Christian standard.

But let none of us forget that the Lord who gave us such holy rights imposed on us great obligations as well. We should remain true and obedient servants of our Heavenly Father to the end of our days. Only one thing can deprive us of these rights to eternal joys—that is, our sinful and unrepentant life.

Oh, let each of us remind his heart that there is nothing more terrible in this world than to kill one's soul forever as one's depraved life closes forever the doors to the Heavenly Kingdom!

Oh, let each of us inspire his heart with fear and trembling to be mindful of that inevitable, final Divine Judgment when we stand trembling before the Righteous Judge with our naked vices and sins, open and secret, such as we here so carefully hide from people, and when in front of our closest and best friends we await the final Righteous Judgment!

Oh, let our heart, while yet it is not too late for any of us, study to bewail our sins with saving tears of repentance, mindful that each of us at one time did not know how to lie, how to conceal evil against another, did not bear in himself even an unkind thought, but now we have become filthy. With our sins we have distorted in ourselves the image of God which was impressed on the immortal soul of each of us and often we live without even noticing it in ourselves.[21]

This was the dilemma in Nikolai's sermons. While they offered respite from the cruel world outside, they inevitably led to personal confrontation with one's own shortcomings. Particularly for an introspective person, to dwell on these subjects would make it impossible to lull the conscience with half-truths and partial answers, to avoid the awful recognition of the realities of one's life. To ponder sincerely such ideas as these would create a growing tension in a life that had made compromise with evil, and one can only wonder for how long such tension could be borne.

Does not this autumn in nature tell us—so powerfully, so clearly—of the autumn of human life, of that autumn into which many of us [here] with you have already entered, and into which those of you who are still going along the same inevitable path to that time will enter? A man's head is covered with silver, all the hitherto hidden illnesses are revealed in all their force, the once erect figure is stooped, arms and legs lose their strength and force, sight becomes clouded, hearing weak, and all the forces of life flicker.

• • •

Of what does autumn tell us? Autumn in nature is a time of ripening of fruits, a time of harvest, a time of reckoning the supplies for the winter until the future spring. Happy the man who gathers from the trees of his own orchard, from the beds of his own garden many fruits, fully ripe, full-blooded, steeped with the dampness of mother earth in their juices. Not in vain were his labors in the growing garden, in tilling the soil. The coming winter does not frighten him.

• • •

Each of us, children of God, should be living stalks in the corn-field of the Christian life; each should become wheat, ready for the unveiling of the eternal, blessed kingdom of heaven for each soul—that kingdom of light, in which there cannot be filth, lies or evil, for "what communion hath light with darkness?" (II Cor. 6:14), as the holy Apostle Paul says. For his whole life the Christian should stand at the door of his heart, not allowing sin into it and struggling with that sin which crawls in the heart as a serpent. For this reason the Christian is given the blessing of confession, which is called a "second baptism," so that when he has overcome sin in himself he may wash thereby, he may cleanse and whiten his immortal soul for eternal life, making his soul worthy of participation in the joys of the eternal kingdom of light. Earthly life is given to each of us for preparing ourselves for the life of the endless future age. The ear of corn must ripen.

And otherwise?

We know the immutable and terrible word of the impartial Eternal Judgment:

"And in the time of harvest I will say to the reapers, Gather ye together first the tares, and bind them in bundles to burn them; . . . The harvest is the end of the world; and the reapers are angels." (Matt. 13:30, 39)

May none of us be in this terrible judgment of the tares!

May our part be in another:

"And I will say to the reapers, . . . Gather the wheat into my barn." (Matt. 13:30)

Oh, it is needful only to be worthy of this happiness! To each of us are given but a few decades for this, to earn this happiness during them.

"Set your affection on things above," the holy Apostle Paul teaches. (Col. 3:2)

In your life do not lower your spiritual gaze from the heights of the high, excellent Heavenly Jerusalem—the place of our eternal habitation! And let the thought of our eternal salvation be first in the line of our other thoughts; let concern for the soul be before all other concerns, and let labor for the greatest task on earth—for the salvation of our soul for eternal bliss—be a life-long labor for each of us. We shall prepare ourselves for the eternal spring of that life which will not know an end!

Beloved elders! Never forget the words of Christ that with the heavenly Master he who comes to him in the eleventh, final hour of his life will receive a like reward to those who came before him.[22]

VIII

The New Era

Early in 1953 Stalin's rule ended. His death was announced on March 5, and four days later Nikolai was among the dignitaries attending his funeral. But it was more than the funeral of a man: Stalin's death marked the end of an era in Soviet history.

The leadership of the USSR immediately became embroiled in a struggle for power, and for several years the political situation in the USSR would be in flux as rival leaders and contending factions sought control. The prominence of Malenkov, the diminishing publicity given to Moscow, the disappearance and then the execution (announced after a six-month delay) of Beria, the rise of Bulganin, and Khrushchev's ascendancy all gave evidence of a quiet, bitter, and violent struggle taking place behind Kremlin walls.[1]

It is difficult to determine what the reaction of the Russian Orthodox Church to these events was. In general, the church probably welcomed the uncertainty in government. With governmental policy in doubt, the church had an opportunity to continue its work more effectively, working quietly to increase its strength in the countryside. With so much doubt at the center of governmental authority, local officials would be less likely to interfere with the conduct of the church, preferring to wait until the policy line had been clarified. For a governmental official to take action during such a time of flux would be unwise, for, whether local officials were firm or lenient in their relation to the Christians, a change in state policy would leave them on the wrong side and responsible to the Party for their actions. Therefore, local governmental officials would be likely to postpone action and, so long as the church conducted its work unobtrusively, it stood to gain strength during the interregnum.

On the patriarchal level, the issue was more uncertain. It is true that a succession crisis offered a possibility of further relaxation of religious policy, and certainly the government would be more amenable to influence, for the contending sides were seeking support wherever it was available. Therefore the church might hope for some beneficial results.

Unfortunately, the Russian Orthodox Church had very little effective influence on the high levels of government at this time. Stalin had been identified with a vicious attack on the church before the war and then with a more lenient attitude thereafter. Hence, his death did not represent a clearcut opportunity for the church, for whether his policies were in general continued or repudiated, religious policy could go either way.[2]

The church's formal contact with the government was through Georgii G. Karpov, head of the Council for the Affairs of the Orthodox Church, but it was uncertain how influential such contact could be. Karpov was in an ambiguous position: Although he was identified with Stalin's

relatively lenient attitude toward the internal life of the
church, he also had a second role as a major general in the
MVD in charge of control of religion; it was thus conceiv-
able that the fall of Beria had decreased what influence he
had on the government.[3]

Nor could Nikolai offer much in the way of cooperation
in foreign policy at this time. Soviet foreign policy was in
some confusion after the death of Stalin, for during the
period of the succession crisis the state could ill afford
international risks. Therefore the church's collaboration in
international affairs would remain a minor issue until a
general Soviet foreign policy had crystalized.

The power of the Russian Orthodox Church to influence
the government was at a minimum, even though the nature
of the political situation made the Soviet leadership especially
susceptible to such influence. The only way in which effective religious influence could be brought to bear on the
leadership would have been from abroad, but expressions of
such concern for the Russian situation by the Western
churches did not materialize until 1956.

There were several reasons for this failure on the part of
Western Christians. Chief among them was the abysmal
ignorance on the part of the overwhelming majority of
Western Christians about the situation of the Russian
churches. Only a minuscule faction of Western Christians—
clergy and laity alike—had more than the haziest knowledge
of Christianity in the USSR, and those church leaders who
were seriously concerned about the situation not only were
relatively few, but, more importantly, their concern was not
reflected among their constituents. Broad support within the
churches, which is a prerequisite for truly effective action,
was missing entirely.

It is not surprising, however, that Western Christians as

a whole were unaware of the possible opportunities during this period. At the time, only a comparatively small number of scholars and very few journalists were at all cognizant of the power struggle within the Kremlin, and few examples of penetrating analysis were all but lost in the flood of rumor, speculation, and imagination, which is the constant bane of the highly speculative science of Kremlinology. The full picture of the power struggle in the USSR was not pieced together until several years after the event, and therefore it would have been a rare churchman indeed who realized the opportunities at hand when many professional analysts of Soviet politics were themselves hardly aware of them.

Finally, even had Western Christians been aware of opportunities, it would have been foolhardy to attempt to exert influence on the Soviet regime without sufficient knowledge, for ill-conceived attempts to do so might very well have backfired, increasing the difficulties of the Russian churches rather than ameliorating their situation.[4] In the mid-fifties there was relatively little competent Western scholarship on the contemporary situation of Russian Christianity. Such a tradition of scholarship as there had been had all but lapsed for a generation, and those leaders who did wish to find an effective expression of their concern were hampered by the vacuum of reliable resources on which they might have drawn in formulating possible approaches to the problem.

In such circumstances it is sometimes better to hesitate rather than to risk inadequately informed action that might end tragically. For if the succession crisis offered hope of a change for the better in religious policy, the converse was also true. Militant atheism exercised a powerful attraction in the Communist Party, especially among the young. The contending factions in the power struggle had to look both to gaining public support and to retaining the support of the

Party in the attempt to overcome rival factions, and it was not altogether unlikely that one faction or another in the power struggle would seek Party support by advocating a return to the antireligious policy of the thirties. There was a strong possibility that greater severity in religious policy might be used to balance deviations from strict communist ideals undertaken in order to win public popularity.

Apparently something like this actually took place. Malenkov had made notable concessions in his attempt to secure power. In economic matters he was identified with an emphasis of consumer production over heavy industry; in foreign affairs his policy had been one of seeking a *détente* with the West, most notably in agreeing to an armistice in Korea and to a resolution of the Austrian question. Both of these policies represented deviations from the accepted canons of Party doctrine.

Concurrently, the Khrushchev faction appeared to be making a determined bid for Party support by identifying itself with a stricter, more unyielding adherence to accepted Party goals. Khrushchev, at the time, seemed more inclined to favor heavy industry than consumer goods, and in agricultural policy he was identified with the introduction (in 1954) of stern measures increasing state control over the collective farms. Both of these measures would tend to place Malenkov in the unenviable position of a "deviationist" from the tenets of the Communist Party.

In 1954 a brief but bitter antireligious campaign, later called the "Hundred Days Campaign," was mobilized. Antireligious propaganda had not been so vitriolic since before the war, and great numbers of attacks on religion were published. The campaign was widely identified with Malenkov,[5] and may have represented an attempt to regain the support of the more militant Communists by balancing his less-rigid approach to economics and foreign policy with an exceedingly rigid approach to religion.

On November 10, 1954, the Central Committee of the Party issued a decree denouncing excesses of the antireligious campaign, which stopped the militant campaign entirely.[6] It was signed by N. S. Khrushchev, the first secretary of the Central Committee. In all probability this decree was primarily a political maneuver (Khrushchev's later actions displayed no great friendliness to religion and no antipathy to intense antireligious activity).[7] This was the first document that Khrushchev had signed personally, and thus it was his first direct assertion of complete, personal control over the Party. Religion was an ideal issue, for it was considered a third-rate concern by most Party members, and Khrushchev's decree was carefully couched in Leninist language. It was most unlikely that anyone would challenge his right to speak for the Party on such an issue. It also served the dual purpose of defeating Malenkov's bid to gain Party support and of gaining for Khrushchev a measure of public good will.

There were reports that church members made it a practice for a long time to carry copies of the decree, which they had clipped from the newspapers, to frustrate actions by local officials against their church.[8] The cessation of the campaign was also a welcome sign to the church's leaders, although it is probable that most leaders—including Nikolai —had sufficient experience with the Kremlin to keep from placing too much faith in the decree.

There were many reports of a revival of religion in Russia during the fifties.[9] The temporary eclipse of the Secret Police and the drastic reduction of its powers within the USSR doubtless resulted in a great deal more freedom of action for the church, and the church took judicious advantage of the eased conditions to increase its strength. The church was quietly gaining strength while the government was engaged in the succession crisis, and such a growth within the church enabled the leaders in the patriarchate to breathe more easily. In particular, Nikolai's position was probably strengthened, for any increase in the influence of the church over the Soviet people would certainly increase his potential effectiveness at the bargaining table with the state. New winds were blowing within the church, winds of confidence and of hope that the long night of state hostility, with its attendant threat of the destruction of the church, might soon be over.

New winds were blowing in Soviet society as well. The most notable index of change appeared in literature and the arts.[10] Hesitantly, and little by little, Soviet artists made a few tentative attempts to move out of the strict confines of state control and to probe a little deeper into the life around them. Of particular importance for the church was the republication of the works of Tolstoy and Dostoyevsky.[11] Many works deeply imbued with Christianity, such as these, had been virtually unobtainable under Stalin. Their return to public circulation had significant effect in Russian Orthodoxy's efforts to strengthen its position among the people.

It would be interesting to know whether Nikolai returned to the works of Tolstoy during this period. Tolstoy was recognized throughout the world as one of the great prophets of pacifism, and many of Nikolai's activities in the Peace Campaign could claim to reflect the thought of Tolstoy in one measure or another. Seen in this light, the Peace Campaign might seem not a device of the Communist Party, but a continuation of the pioneering work of a Russian Christian. This might have resolved some of the dilemma of Christian collaboration with a movement promoted by the atheistic state.

Ironically, however, Tolstoy had been excommunicated by the Russian Orthodox Church. Much of his work on pacifism would be considered by the church to reflect heretical Christianity. And, indeed, it is fully possible that Nikolai did not have occasion to reflect at all on Tolstoy's significance for the Peace Campaign, for the fact that Tolstoy was excommunicated might have influenced Nikolai's literary tastes somewhat.

In 1955 and 1956 the great emancipation from the labor camps took place,[12] and this event may have had a profound effect on the life of Nikolai. The rapid de-emphasis of the Secret Police within Russia, which accompanied Khrushchev's rise to power, necessitated a decreasing emphasis if not a complete renunciation of reliance on forced labor as an integral part of the Soviet economy. From the early thirties onward a large forced-labor force had been maintained by the state under the almost independent administration of the Secret Police.[13] Exact figures of its size are unavailable, but informed estimates of its peak population range between seven and twelve million forced laborers in penal camps. The forced-labor system may have accounted for as much as one-sixth of the state budget at its peak. Much of Soviet domestic fishing,[14] forestry,[15] and mining[16] was accomplished by forced labor, as well as the great majority of large-scale public works projects (such as canals), especially in the far north.

A large number of the forced laborers were Christians, many of whom had been arrested because of their religious activities.[17] Many bishops, thousands of priests, and millions of Orthodox laymen had been exiled to the labor camps. The vast majority of them may be presumed to have died, for the normal sentence for "political" offenses after the war was ten to twenty-five years of "corrective labor," and the average life expectancy at some of the worst camps was three to five years.

But by 1956 people were beginning to return from the camps, benefactors of large-scale amnesty granted by the state as it closed down most of the camps. Churchmen were among those returning. Some of these returning churchmen were known by Nikolai personally, and it is entirely possible that in 1956 he met again with fellow bishops who had disappeared years before. Many who served sentences at forced labor were permanently broken in health, and the marginal subsistence at the camps left a visible mark on all of the laborers. If a person's appearance itself bore testimony to the harshness of conditions in the camps, how much more would intimate conversation with such a person reveal the barbarity of the forced-labor system![18]

One of the abilities of the Soviet populace—and probably one of the reasons Stalin was able to impose his rule so effectively—is an ability to maintain a safe degree of ignorance.[19] People in Russia during the Stalin years knew very well that evil things were happening—friends were arrested, people disappeared, fraudulent court trials were published, police agents were always watching and listening—but they managed to conduct their day-to-day lives without thinking about these things. With one part of their mind they knew, and yet, the basic need to survive tended to submerge this knowledge. So great was the inner insulation from this uncomfortable—and exceedingly dangerous—knowledge that on the rare occasions of conscious realization of these barbarities the honest reaction would be shock.

It should not be supposed that this willing ignorance was confined to the uneducated masses. To the contrary, it probably operated most effectively among the educated sections of the population. Certainly something of this insulation often exists in the thinking of members of the Communist Party. It may be that such an unwillingness to recognize unpleasant fact is a byproduct of modern totalitarianism itself. It is not at all unlikely that Nikolai succumbed to this bifurcation of separating knowledge from recognition of the knowledge.

The return of the emancipated exiles, however, shattered this comfortable ignorance. Nobody could have met an old friend returned from the labor camps without coming face to face with the unpleasant, shocking reality. The illusions which had been so carefully nurtured would be shattered, and one would be forced against his will to face up to at least a part of the awful reality of what Soviet rule had meant in Russia.

The return of the prelates and priests may have had a special impact on Nikolai. Most of them had suffered imprisonment rather than compromise their faith. While they had been at the camps Nikolai had been free. Their reappearance may have raised again in Nikolai's mind the question of the price with which his own freedom had been won, and might have revived the larger issue of justifying his willingness to collaborate with the state in order to purchase conditions for the survival of the church, while other prelates had suffered for refusing that price. The return of the exiles may have confronted Nikolai with some very disturbing questions indeed.

A more devastating revelation took place in the USSR in 1956. At the Twentieth Party Congress in February, Khrushchev made his famous "Secret Speech," which denounced Stalin and began the de-Stalinization campaign.[20] The United States obtained a copy, and because the speech had been published in the West, the basic outlines of the speech finally became known by the Soviet populace.

The revelation of the crimes of Stalin had a tremendous impact within Russia, for it shattered the illusion so carefully built by the state during the Stalin years, an illusion that ascribed to Stalin a virtual infallibility, creating the image of an all-wise, beneficent, fatherly ruler. Just as it would no longer be possible for Nikolai to retain illusions when confronted by the released convict laborers, so the Russian people at large could no longer maintain their customary illusions about Stalin and the Stalinist state.

Before the fall of tsarism, one of the great frustrations of the liberal and radical reformers was the inexplicable faith of the Russian people in the tsar. The people referred to the tsar as the "little father," thinking of him in terms of reverent fealty, despite the fact that many of the tsars were uncommonly tyrannical.[21] Russians knew a great deal about corruption in local politics, but somehow they did not suspect that such corruption could exist at the head of the state. The many injustices of the tsarist regime were ascribed to the bureaucracy, and that they were not rectified was assumed to be due to the fact that the tsar's corrupt officials kept him from knowing the true facts. Perhaps the fall of the monarchy was due in part to the final dissolution of this myth of the perfect beneficence of the tsar.

Inexplicably, this same attitude seems to have carried over into postrevolutionary society. Apparently, the myth of Stalin's perfection was genuinely believed by large segments of the Soviet population, and the tyrannies of daily life were the fault of corrupt bureaucrats, not of the leader of the state, they thought.

Even among the unfortunates who inhabited the forced-labor camps, there was a large measure of faith in Stalin. Innocents who had been gratuitously arrested, brutally interrogated, and unjustly sentenced often felt that if only their case could be brought to Stalin's attention, the injustices of the Secret Police would be corrected and they would be freed. Prisoners devoted great energy to quixotic attempts to reach Stalin with pleas, for Stalin still bore the mantle of the "little father" for a great many Soviet citizens.

This attitude appears to have been particularly common in the lower ranks of the Communist Party. Stalin's public utterances were firmly committed to the great ideals of Marxism, and the brutalities committed in the name of the Party surely must be due to imperfections within the bureaucracy. The illusion of Stalin as the perfect, all-wise, infallible Leader probably helped to keep the Party intact during the years of terror.

Khrushchev's denunciation of Stalin destroyed this illusion. If the tyranny had not been a deviation from Party norms, but had been instigated by the Leader himself, then could it be possible that the Party was not committed to the just and humane ideals of Marxism but was merely a vehicle for inhuman dictatorship? One of the chief problems to confront Khrushchev throughout the de-Stalinization campaign was how to keep the denunciation of the leader from spreading into a renunciation of the system as a whole.

The church was a direct beneficiary of the de-Stalinization campaign. Great numbers of people lost faith in communism and returned to the Christian church. This was particularly true among the young, for many of the young idealists were committed to the Party because of their faith in the promised goodness and justice of the communist system. When Stalin fell and it became evident that the Party had been responsible for monstrous cruelties and miscarriages of justice, many young people were left without an adequate answer to their deep commitment. The Christian church alone seemed able to meet their need. The god had failed. When the god fell, many of the people turned to God.[22]

It is difficult to determine the effect of the de-Stalinization trauma on Nikolai. Whether or not he also had fallen under the spell of Stalinism is not known. It is altogether possible that he, with the masses of the Russian people, had come under the influence of the Stalin myth to some degree. He knew very well that communism was atheistic and fundamentally evil in many of its practices, but he may have felt that Stalin, like a tsar, was somehow different from the system, that he was more just, more humane, and less hostile to Christianity than were his corrupt officials. Nikolai had made many references to Stalin during the years and had been lavish in his praise of the Leader. Although he may have been merely conforming to the required ritual, many of his paeans of praise to Stalin are fully consonant with an inner acceptance of the general myth of Stalinism.

Whatever the case, the denunciation of Stalin must have confronted Nikolai with a considerable dilemma. If he had succumbed to the Stalin myth, that myth was shattered. If he had not, he would be faced with the enormity of his actions in praise of Stalin, wherein he, as a Christian, had joined in praising Stalin in terms that even the Communists themselves were now rejecting.

In summary, life in the Soviet Union began to change drastically after the death of Stalin. Questions were being asked, doubts were being raised. To be sure, it was a relatively slow process, and daily life by 1956 was far from free and open. But an attitude of re-evaluation and questioning was developing. Patterns of life that had been habitual during the Stalin period were no longer quite so comfortable, and what had seemed reasonable and proper, a normal way of doing things, now became doubtful.

In such an atmosphere it seems unlikely that the church's attitude toward the state could escape a renewed questioning. The old dilemma of whether it is right for the church to collaborate with an atheistic state might again come under examination in the minds of many of those involved in the day-to-day conduct of this policy. Questions that had lain dormant for years, that had once been answered in terms of the Stalin period, might have risen again as the new winds of change brought a demand for revision of earlier attitudes toward Stalin and his regime.

For Soviet society was slowly emerging from its cocoon. The medieval rule of Stalin, which had tried to seal Russia off from the outside world, had dissolved, and the chrysalis of the emerging society found itself thrust without preparation into the twentieth century. The authoritarian framework, with its unquestioned dogmas and single pattern of thought, with its simplistic, black-and-white worldview and its facile schema of right and wrong, was crumbling, and Soviet citizens found themselves confronted with the confusing modern world, where there are no simple answers, where doubt and uncertainty abound, and where alienation and despair are ever-present dangers. During the few short years after the death of Stalin, Soviet society suddenly began to emerge into the twentieth century. An era had ended.

In 1956, an exchange of church delegations between the National Council of Churches of the United States and the Russian Orthodox Church took place. This was an unprecedented event and had a profound effect on the subsequent history of the relations between the Christians of the two countries. More specifically, this exchange may have had a crucial effect on Nikolai's own life.

Considering the strained relations between the United States and the USSR during the first half of the fifties, that such an exchange could take place at all was a rather remarkable achievement. The visit of the American churchmen had required a full year of negotiations, and the initial attempt to work out an exchange had taken place some four years before the actual visits.

When a desire for this sort of an exchange was first made known to the U.S. Department of State, the United States was unwilling to grant permission for the trip. The Korean War was still in process, and tension between the United States and the Soviet Union was still exceedingly high. When the State Department did acquiesce to the idea a short time later, the Soviet government was unwilling. The matter was reopened in 1955 and the applications were accepted this time, but long and difficult negotiations over such matters as details of the visits, composition of the delegations, and the agendas had to be concluded before the American delegation was finally able to visit the USSR in the spring of 1956.

The exchange of delegations was an expression of a long history of American Protestant concern for the ecumenical dimensions of the faith. As early as April 1941, American Christians had met with Japanese Christians in order to affirm their solidarity despite the growing tension between the two countries in international politics. Immediately after World War II this feeling of a Christian solidarity that transcends political differences was given concrete expression when missions were sent by the American churches to Germany and Japan to aid in the rehabilitation of the Christian churches in those countries.

Many of the Christian leaders intimately involved in these early expressions of the ecumenical movement felt—and still feel—that a demonstration of Christian solidarity across the frontiers of major political enmity was one of the most im-

portant, or indeed, the most important aspect, of ecu-
menicity: the refusal to allow political divisions to separate
Christians.

With the beginning of the fifties the rehabilitation of the
German and Japanese churches was progressing well. But
the Cold War had introduced new enmities between the
United States and the USSR, and, although armed hostility
between these major world powers had not yet occurred,
the division between the two nations—and between the
Christians of the two nations—appeared to be fully as serious
as those that had divided the belligerents in the preceding
war.

For this reason, the American churchmen were actively
concerned with making contact with their Russian counter-
parts. Obviously, there was need for communication among
Christians between whom political differences had raised a
barrier. The Americans felt that serious misunderstandings
had arisen. Concerned less with misinterpretations of the
motivations and attitudes of American Christians expressed
by representatives of Russian Orthodoxy than with the
larger problem of divergent interpretations of world history
and international events on the part of Christians of the two
countries, the Americans felt it imperative that personal
contact be made between representatives of the two Christian communities in order that a beginning might be made
toward finding grounds for mutual understanding. The
Americans knew that the Russian Orthodox spokesmen,
chief among whom was Nikolai, had misinterpreted; they
wished a personal meeting to establish a basis on which these
misinterpretations could be overcome by mutual understanding.[23]

The clearest expression of many of these misinterpretations and misunderstandings, of course, was to be found in

the foreign activities of the Russian church and, specifically, in some of the more propagandistic of Nikolai's speeches. Thus it was the Department of External Relations, with Nikolai as its head, that felt the primary impact of the exchange. Coming as it did at a time when many of the old values and patterns of Russian life were in flux, the confrontation may have had a profound effect on Nikolai's personal life as well.

The crucial event in the American visit came when the council leaders engaged Nikolai in a closed session of frank discussion.[24] It was during this discussion that the inaccurate and unfair statements Nikolai had made about the West and the churches of the West in the course of his propaganda were called into question.

The choice of the American churchmen for this confrontation was the germ warfare issue, which indicated no little insight on their part. Because this issue was no longer being promoted by Soviet propaganda, Nikolai might not be required to support the claim, and thus it seemed a reasonably good issue to focus upon. The position taken by the Americans was that talk of closer relations was impossible so long as false accusations, as exemplified by the germ warfare charges, remained unresolved.

It was a dramatically tense discussion. The Americans assumed that it was being monitored secretly by the agents of the state, so they expected that Nikolai probably would not be able to discuss the matter with them in that simple frankness that might be his preferred idiom as a churchman, as Christian to Christian, and without ambiguity. Nikolai's attempts to brush the issue aside, however, were in vain, and the Americans persisted relentlessly in pressing the issue.

Nikolai, and the Russian church, appeared to be very desirous of closer relations with Western churches. But

Nikolai was on the horns of a dilemma. He was unable to evade the issue by claiming he had been misunderstood, for the Americans had brought with them translations from the *Journal of the Moscow Patriarchate*, in which the issue was specifically raised, and could point to the printed page to support their charge.[25] (It was a minor irony that the only reference to bacteriological warfare in the selections from Nikolai's speeches included in the translated excerpts was from the speech of December 1950, in which Nikolai disapprovingly quoted the American professor's statement, "I approve bacteriological war, the use of gas. . . ."[26] However, Nikolai as editor of the *Journal* was rightly accountable for its contents by other authors, many of whom were much more specific in their charges.)

Quite obviously, the charge of germ warfare was unacceptable to the Americans. Nikolai could not admit that the charge may have been inaccurate, for to do so would be to accuse the Soviet state of dishonesty. He certainly could not hope to explain the extraordinarily complex situation between church and state in the USSR, which might make such concessions to the demands of state propaganda understandable if not entirely justifiable. Not only would such an attempt bring down the wrath of the state, which maintains the fiction that full freedom of religion exists in the Soviet Union, but it also would have been highly unlikely that Nikolai could have communicated this exceedingly complicated relationship to all the Americans present in one short sitting.

The dialogue placed Nikolai in an intolerable position. His face became red, and it was plainly visible that he was in terrible embarrassment. His manner on this occasion was completely unlike his normal poise and composure. The only response he could give was the statement that was later released to the press: "I think that the question refers to such a period of the distant past that it is not useful to discuss. Now we are seeking ways of understanding each other better, of growing closer to each other."[27]

Such a position was not satisfactory to the American churchmen. Not only was four years too recent to be considered the "distant past," but such issues were at present the primary impediment to closer relations. After the American delegation had reminded Metropolitan Nikolai that "there can be no forgiveness without repentance," the conversation finally terminated with the issue unresolved.

The Americans expressed no judgment on Nikolai's personal reactions during the conversation, but reported that he was exceedingly agitated and embarrassed. Whether this confrontation involved him in a direct, personal confrontation with the ethical enormity of many of his accusations must remain uncertain.

It probably struck Nikolai as quite ironic that the issue chosen by the Americans was that of germ warfare. As we have seen, Nikolai had not been particularly enthusiastic about that aspect of the PEACE CAMPAIGN. It might have surprised him that the Americans had chosen this minor matter, when there were so many aspects of his public life much more vulnerable to criticism. However, the Americans had made it plain, and Nikolai was doubtless intelligent enough to see, that this specific issue served merely to focus the multitude of questionable allegations Nikolai had made about the West and its Christians over the years.

Even though his answer that the events occurred in the "distant past" was unacceptable to the Americans, it was a good answer, probably a great deal better than Nikolai himself realized at the time. Even if fortuitously, the answer contained an exceedingly intelligent appraisal of recent events in Russia. For the events had indeed occurred in the distant past, in a different era entirely. These were events from the medieval period of Stalinism, and were far removed from the current situation, in which church and society were struggling to emerge into modern times. To revive the gross propaganda rubrics of the Stalin period was irrelevant in the subtle Khrushchevian context of the new era. It was a penetrating answer to the American charges, and had the visiting churchmen themselves been Russian, had they lived through the preceding quarter of a century of Stalin's rule, and had they known more of what was happening within the USSR than the few bits and pieces that managed to filter through the regime's policy of secrecy, it might have satisfied them as a subtle but perfectly acceptable answer.

To repeat, it is impossible to determine whether or not this conversation led Nikolai to personal re-evaluation of his actions, to a point of inner crisis. But apparently something did happen to change Nikolai's life in 1956. There is a noticeable change in his activity from 1956 onward, and Western church leaders who had personal contact with Nikolai are convinced that the exchange of visits with the American churchmen played no small role in effecting that change.[28] The genuine concern displayed by the American churches, their degree of honesty and openness despite political division, and perhaps the focal point of this one confrontation on the germ warfare issue could very well have served to precipitate the change in Nikolai.

Whatever its causes, there is a difference in his work from 1956 on. While he still participated in the propaganda activities of the state, the tone of his later utterances is entirely different from those we have already reviewed in connection with the PEACE CAMPAIGN. Gone is the extremism, the disregard for balance and truth, the stridency and lack of restraint. Nikolai's later propaganda is much more careful and seems much more sensitive to ethics. It is possible that his later speeches reflect a genuine inner change in Nikolai's attitude.

Unfortunately, however, the issue is not entirely clear. Soviet propaganda as a whole was undergoing a metamorphosis, as the extremism of the Stalin era was replaced by the more subtle effectiveness of the Khrushchevian period. It may be that the change in tone in Nikolai's works after 1956 was not indicative of a genuine conversion or change of attitude, but merely reflected the changed demands of state propaganda as a whole.

Even with a change in style of Soviet propaganda, some of Nikolai's activities after his confrontation with Western Christians in 1956 seemed astonishingly irenic. A case in point was his statement after the Hungarian revolution in November 1956. It will be recalled that the Red Army had crushed the revolt, and so shocking was the Soviet disregard of the norms of international morality that great numbers of Western Communists left the Party in protest.[29]

The Soviet justification for its action consisted in the claim that the revolt was inspired by foreign capitalists; therefore, the Red Army, in crushing the revolt, was only protecting the true interests of the people.

Late in November Eugene Carson Blake, who had been chairman of the American delegation to Russia in 1956, sent a telegram to the patriarchate asking for aid to the Hungarians. Nikolai's reply was:

With all our hearts we join our prayers to yours that the world may find a just solution of problems in the Middle East without further violence or bloodshed.

Our Government is giving material aid to those who suffer in Hungary. In this our churches are participating. We shall devotedly and unceasingly labor for peace as the final goal of the Kingdom of God on earth.[30]

The mention of the Middle East (which implied that actions of some of the Western governments in the Suez crisis might also be subject to debate) was the most Nikolai allowed himself to contribute to the polemics then raging in the political sphere, and he had nothing more to say about Hungary in his reply. This reticence was truly remarkable when compared with Nikolai's former habits.

Further signs of relaxation, or at least radical change, in the foreign activities undertaken by the Russian church were evident in its relationship to the World Council of Churches. At its inception that body had extended an open invitation to the Russian Orthodox Church to join in the movement, and the door had not been closed despite the tensions of the Cold War.[31] At the conclusion of a visit to the USSR by a delegation from the World Council of Churches in 1958, Nikolai announced to the press that he would recommend that his church join.[32] Though he did not belittle the problems that remained to be solved, such as differing views on a nuclear test ban, Nikolai said, "There is no doubt, however, that this first meeting has been a good basis for future contacts and meetings."

A year later, in a message of greeting to the Central Committee of the World Council of Churches, Nikolai stated:

We Christians must stand above the political contradictions of our time and give to the divided peoples an example of unity, of peace, of brotherhood and of love, removing ourselves from all self-sufficient isolationism, and of friendly relations to each other.

We Orthodox Christians are in great sympathy with the ecumenical movement because we believe that our western brothers honestly aim at overcoming the destructive separation in faith.[33]

The profound difference between this statement and the earlier attitudes expressed by Nikolai is obvious. Had the next two years of Nikolai's life allowed his continuation in office, he would doubtless be remembered as the Russian churchman most intimately involved in the entry of Russian Orthodoxy into the ecumenical movement, for, in fact, Nikolai was the primary Russian representative involved in the negotiations that took place after the confrontation of 1956, negotiations that in five years would bring the Russian Orthodox Church into membership in the World Council of Churches. This unprecedented change in policy presented to the world a complete break with the tradition Nikolai had exemplified before 1956.

It seemed to be a different Nikolai who came to the United States on the return visit in June of 1956.[34] Whatever reserve or suspicion might have been detected in his bearing when he arrived quickly dissipated, and Nikolai conducted himself on his tour of the world of American Protestantism with great dignity and openness. He seemed to harbor none of the hostility to Western Christianity and none of the onesided extremism that had characterized so much of his activities in the PEACE CAMPAIGN.

During his stay in the United States Nikolai delivered a remarkable sermon at the (patriarchal) St. Nicholas Orthodox Church in New York. It was a sermon that bore no resemblance whatsoever to his previous utterances designed for foreign consumption. According to a reporter of *The New York Times*:

The Russian clergyman declared that "Holy Russia" would never die. He said that thousands of years hence the church and its God would survive, "nourished by the Holy Russian soil and the faith of the Russian people."

There was no word of communism and no reference to the Soviet Government in the Metropolitan's sermon. Nor did he discuss the world peace movement or international policy. He spoke solely of the universal church and almost exclusively of the church in Russia.

• • •

"Preserve your faith," the clergyman said, "and your guardian angel will protect you. Jesus Christ will never desert you."

He declared that in Russia today churches were open and overflowing, not just on the high feast days, the holidays, and the ceremonials, but every day in the week.

Russians, he said, make pilgrimages of thousands of miles to visit the great church shrines, such as the Kiev lavra, or monastery, and the great Troitza monastery near Moscow.

"The holy spirit of Christ protects us and will save us," he declared. "The most priceless and valued possession is the belief of our people."[35]

It would probably be unwise to attach too much significance to Nikolai's conduct on his visit to the United States. His moderate tone may have been indicative of a genuine change in attitude. However, Khrushchev's Russia was seeking expanded contact with the West, and the lack of militancy in Nikolai's conduct could have been due to the change in state policy. Whether or not a change had actually occurred in Nikolai's inner life, it is also true that his conduct in the United States conformed to the requirements of Soviet foreign policy at the moment.

But the sermon at St. Nicholas Cathedral was significant, not so much in its content, but rather in the course of events that would cause the ideas in that sermon to be repeated three years later in Moscow. In his sermon in New York,

Nikolai was consciously or unconsciously predicting an event of crucial significance for his own life.

Perhaps there was also a prophetic note in the message he delivered on his patron saint's day in 1956, designed not for foreign consumption but for the Russian believers in Moscow. Speaking before hundreds of Russian Orthodox, many of whom were among his most intimate associates, Nikolai said:

We Christians, when we do anything, should think what the Lord teaches, that we do only that which we should do. Therefore I ask you to pray that in the remaining time of my life I might do what I have not done but should have done as an archpastor of the Orthodox Church.[36]

IX

The Pastor: Patriotism and Martyrdom

THE DEEP ATTACHMENT to Mother Russia, evident in Nikolai's sermon in New York in 1956, echoes a strong theme of Nikolai's sermons. They reflect an attachment to Orthodoxy which was deeply intertwined with patriotism, a love of native land. One of the major assets of Russian Orthodoxy is its ability to draw on the natural patriotism of the Russian people, and Nikolai's sermons reflect this deeply emotional attraction in full measure.

We know how sublime, sacred, is the feeling of patriotism. This feeling of unlimited love of native land is deeply rooted in the spiritual nature of the Slav. . . .

The Russian from century to century lived and lives with this powerful, and at the same time tender, love of his native land. But with us believers, as we have said, this love towards our native land becomes a Christian duty: it is illuminated with the evangelical light of Christ's commandments.[1]

It should be noted, however, that this form of patriotism differs somewhat from the artificial creation which is Soviet patriotism. The substitute, which the Communist regime sought to parade as the genuine article, was effective only to the extent that it was able to identify with the deeper patriotism of the Russian people. Therefore it would be grossly mistaken to confuse Nikolai's many expressions of loyalty to the Soviet government in his public activities with the deeper, more mysterious patriotism of his sermons.

It is instructive to note that Nikolai's graduation into public leadership involved precisely the issue of Russian patriotism. It was in mobilizing the natural patriotism of the Russian people to the aid of the war effort that Nikolai made his first publicized act of service to the state. And it would also be the issue of patriotism that would be involved in his departure from public life.

The entire structure of Russian Orthodoxy expresses Russian patriotism. Even the church buildings, with their ancient architecture, appeal to the great history and traditions of "Old Russia."

Why have Orthodox Russian people so loved to build their temples from the times of ancient *Rus?* In the first ages of our Christianity in *Rus*, it was for our forebears a testament of special love to God to build temples in the course of one or two days. Such a temple was built "by the whole world." We middle-aged people remember from the days of our childhood and youth the many collectors for the temple who stood on the grounds of our churches and visited honorable people at home for the collection of offerings for building temples. . . . This is why sincere Orthodox Russian people also love to decorate their temples with gold, with silver, with bright paint, with embroideries, with flowers. This love for decorating our temples does not die and cannot die in the heart of a believing person. How can we not beautify that place in which we meet with the Lord, in which He Himself always is present in His Holy Sacraments?[2]

In other words, all of the activities within the church are intertwined with love of the Russian country. To be Orthodox meant to be *Russian* Orthodox, and every aspect of the faith was bound up in the deep patriotism of being Russian. Even the icons of the church generated an appeal to patriotism, and their contemplation elicited that same deep emotion that connected the person to his native land.

Orthodox countries know many wonder-working icons of the Mother of God. In unique measure our country, our holy *Rus*, is watered by these holy icons. It was not by coincidence that our forebears called our *Rus* the Home of the Mother of God. Even before we saw light She loved us, and gave to our Church, to our native land these countless pledges of Her stay with us. And even in our infancy and childhood our believing parents led and bore us to these wonder-working holy things, they entrusted the Mother of God [icon] with care and covering, and, before we ourselves consciously began to go to Her, She had already blessed us, was already caressing us through these holy icons.[3]

Devotion to the icons gave expression to Orthodoxy's great emphasis on the lives of the saints of the church. Many of the saints had played a significant role in the governing of the land, and it may be that Nikolai saw in the lives of the saints the precedent that would justify his own interaction with the government.

He [St. Sergius] was a dispenser and ever-fresh source of love. For this love and his kindness, the Orthodox people came to him from all the ends of the Russian land for thousands of miles. In the name of this love he went to a whole series of Russian cities on foot with a staff in his hands, pacifying the separated princes between themselves and with the great prince of Moscow.

Throughout his whole life he bore his heart blemished by

nothing, preserving the crystal cleanliness of spirit and body. He passionately loved his Native Land which was suffering in his days from the cruel Tatar occupation. As a fiery patriot of his country he blessed the great prince Dmitrii for battle with the Tatars, and at the time of these battles he knelt and with tears prayed God for His heavenly help for the fate of his land of birth.[4]

If Nikolai had been able to view his wartime collaboration with the Communist state in the light of St. Sergius, surely as the postwar years unfolded and Nikolai's services to the state took him ever further from the ideal there may have been an inward unrest and yearning, for the patriotism elicited by the saints would remain.

St. Sergius embodied in himself the best properties of the Russian soul and Russian honor; he was the perfect picture of Christian virtues. As a saint he belonged to the Universal Orthodox Church, but he was a Russian saint, our national hero, and we take pride in him. We regard with admiration that which he gave birth to and educated—the Russian people, to which we belong, and the Orthodox faith which we also profess, the Holy Russian Church whose children we remain. He is our glory, he is our praise! By his life, by the radiant beauty of his submissive heart he calls all of us to imitation. He inspires us also to peace in the name of God and in the name of the soul's salvation.[5]

Nikolai's sermons are often filled with a deep love of the Russian land and the Russian people. During the war this love of Russia doubtless supplied a great emotional force that buttressed Nikolai's service to the government in its hour of peril. One can only wonder, though, whether in the new climate after Stalin's death, with its terrible revelations about the true nature of Stalin's rule, this patriotic devotion to Russia might not eventually turn the other way, might not induce Nikolai to turn against the government that had brought such terror to the Russian land, such suffering to the Russian people.

Nikolai continued his customary service to the state after 1956. Through the next three years he continued to work as the head of the Department of Foreign Affairs of the Russian Orthodox Church. In his position as editor of the *Journal of the Moscow Patriarchate*, he continued to conform to the limitations imposed by the state in its policy of a controlled press.

Nikolai continued to participate in the PEACE CAMPAIGN, but his propaganda, as has been noted, was strangely muted, and without the fire of his earlier peace propaganda. In large measure, this change in tone may simply have reflected the difficulties that had beset the PEACE CAMPAIGN as a whole during this period. Because of their obvious political bias, the Soviet-inspired peace groups had fallen into eclipse after 1954.[6] Their effectiveness was drastically reduced as fewer and fewer people in the West could be convinced that the movement was sincere and free, rather than an arm of Soviet political machination. The PEACE CAMPAIGN was virtually isolated, and hence the state may have desired the muted quality evident in Nikolai's peace activities. Whatever the reason, Nikolai's activities as a whole did seem to be more cautious, more reflective during the years following 1956.

Nikolai was familiar with the works of Dostoyevsky, and the republication of Dostoyevsky in the mid-fifties may have prompted Nikolai to return again to that deeply religious author during this relatively quiescent period in his life. There was much in Dostoyevsky that might have led Nikolai to ponder.

One of the great themes in Dostoyevsky's works, which appears again and again throughout his novels and stories, is the theme of suffering. Suffering and life itself seem to be equated. Only through suffering does one achieve true knowledge of the self, and without suffering there is no growth, no movement, no self-awareness. Complacence is spiritual death.

Dostoyevsky's emphasis on suffering repeats a major theme of Russian Orthodoxy itself. The first Russian saints, Boris and Gleb, the patron saints of the Russian land, were venerated precisely because they suffered death, accepting it as the sufferings of Christ in their lives.[7] Suffering, according to Russian Orthodox tradition, is an essential part of the Christian life.

In Dostoyevsky's treatment of suffering, it becomes a path to expiation, perhaps the only path to atonement for evil. In *Crime and Punishment* Raskolnikov, the murderer, finally accepts arrest and exile voluntarily, confessing to his crime in order to receive the cleansing of suffering. Myskin, in *The Idiot*, chooses to suffer with Ragoshin, the murderer, hoping that in choosing guiltless suffering he can somehow help to atone for the sins of the entire world. Father Zosima, in *The Brothers Karamazov*, takes on himself the guilt of all, and Dmitrii, although innocent of his father's murder, willingly accepts punishment for it, realizing that his inner attitude toward his father makes him guilty. For all of these characters of Dostoyevsky's creation, suffering is the only path of expiation, just as it had been Dostoyevsky's own sufferings in Siberia that had led him to the Orthodox faith.

Nikolai was familiar with Dostoyevsky. And Nikolai had seen the return of those who had suffered for the faith in the penal camps. Certainly, then, Nikolai was exposed to the idea of suffering as necessary to the Christian life and as the path of expiation for sin.

Nikolai also knew of martyrdom. In a sermon he had once said:

We not only glorify the holy martyrs as bearers of the highest feats and undecaying spiritual beauty—we look on them as our teachers also. Of course, we cannot imitate them in their feats of martyrdom: our Lord calls none of us to this feat, but we can and we should imitate their faith, their love, their hope.[8]

The liturgical calendar of the Orthodox church often celebrates martyred saints; thus, Nikolai's pastoral duties made it inevitable that he would have to be thoroughly familiar with martyrdom. His sermons often returned to this subject, and in them one can perhaps see a peculiar attraction toward martyrdom, an attraction that, like Dostoyevsky's emphasis on suffering, echoed an attitude prominent throughout the history of the Russian church.

Soon after the ascension of the Lord Jesus Christ into heaven, not far from the gates of Jerusalem a horrible sight could be seen: a man was being stoned to death. People were throwing stones at him with cruelty, with scorn and insults. The man stood flowing with blood until he fell. His eyes were lifted up to heaven and his bloody dying lips repeated the same prayer with which the Savior died on the cross: "Lord, hold not this sin against them." (Acts 7:60) This was the first martyr, Archdeacon Stephen. God led him to love his neighbor as himself. He died for Christ. He thirsted for his eternal salvation and, wishing the same for his executioners, he prayed for the forgiveness of their sins.

This is true love to one's neighbor. This is true faith in Him Who promised to take each of His true servants to Himself at the end of their earthly path.[9]

In another sermon martyrdom again is presented as a positive attraction, as the noblest expression of the ideal to which the truly Christian life aspires.

You know that all the apostles except for John the Divine finished their apostolic feats with a martyr's death, and the Apostle John the Divine, dying in extreme age, suffered persecutions and tortures. All the apostles in their preaching activity suffered a multitude of all sorts of tortures. They were beaten, incarcerated in dungeons, driven from city to city. Often attempts were made to kill them. But nothing stopped them in their endeavor to continue their apostolic work of preaching to the end of their days. More than that: the holy Apostle Paul, who suffered persecution more than the other Apostles, as though in the person of all said in his epistles: "In all things approving ourselves as the ministers of God in much patience, in afflictions, in necessities . . . in stripes, in imprisonments, in tumults . . . as sorrowful yet always rejoicing." (II Cor. 6:4–10)

From the lives of the holy martyrs we know how the martyrs of the first centuries of Christianity suffered and died. They endured heavy trials before death and, as the legends of the feats of Saint Kathryn, Saint Theodora, Saint Stratilata and many others tell us, as they stood before the face of death with their nails pulled out, with bones broken, with their body burned, they met death smiling. From whence this radiant smile of joy? All from the same source. Suffering and dying, they saw with their eyes of faith the hand of Him extended toward them for whom they died, and in this hand they saw crowns prepared for them according to the promise of the Lord: "Be thou faithful unto death and I will give thee a crown of Life." (Rev. 2:10)[10]

Perhaps Nikolai's attention to martyrdom was merely the fulfillment of a requirement of the church calendar. Yet his sermons seem fully aware of the positive attraction that this highest achievement of Christian heroism could exercise over the believer. It would be difficult indeed for any Christian, however diluted his faith, when confronted with Nikolai's sermons on martyrdom to avoid a genuine response to the heroism and self-sacrifice so vividly portrayed.

Here is one of these cases. It happened in Carthage in the middle of the Third Century. The ruler of the city had undertaken a persecution against Christians and on one of the days he ordered all Christians to gather at the city square. The Christians knew that they were gathering for execution. On one of these streets on the way to the square, a group of heathens saw a woman hurrying along in the direction of this square with a youngster in her arms. They stopped the woman and said to her, "Where are you going?" She answered, "I am a Christian and I am hurrying to the square where all the Christians are gathering." "Can it be that you do not know that all the Christians will be executed?" "I know this and therefore I am hurrying." "But at least leave the youngster at home. Let the innocent child be saved," some, even of the heathens, begged her. "No," cried out the woman, "I wish that my child today would be with me with the Lord." Such an irresistible "thirst" for the Lord in a believing soul![11]

Martyrdom, suffering, patriotism—all were joined together in Nikolai's sermons. The sermons return again and again to the subject of martydrom, finding in it a pattern, an ideal to be praised, perhaps to be sought, in modern life. At least in Nikolai's sermons, there is a deep conviction that martyrdom, the greatest act of faith, is the high, holy goal of life. Even as early as 1946, in a sermon on the martyr saints, he had said:

Would the deeds of our heroes who have given their young lives in the late war for our well-being, for our peaceful life, for our Country, ever die in the memory of the people? Can it be that we will ever forget them? Their deeds are covered with immortal glory. And for what did our holy martyrs, our glory, our pride, die? They died for Christ. They died for the sake of the holy goal of our earthly life—the salvation of the immortal soul. And their deeds were completely voluntary. They had the choice: either to bow down to heathen idols and receive freedom and material well-being or to accept tortures, and they chose the latter.[12]

X

The Break

ONE OF THE minor tragedies of modern Russian history is the life of A. A. Osipov. Osipov was a priest of the Russian Orthodox Church who, until 1959, occupied the chair of Old Testament at the Leningrad Theological Academy. He was a capable man and an able student of the Old Testament, fully equipped to expound on the Scriptures from the traditional Russian Orthodox point of view.[1] As such, he was a valuable asset to the clergy of the postwar church, for after three decades without facilities for theological education, competent professors for the academies were relatively rare.

Unfortunately, Osipov's personal life fell short of the canonical requirements for the priesthood. Russian priests may marry before ordination, but are rigidly prohibited from remarrying if the wife dies. Osipov's marital life was one of the casualties of World War II, however, for his wife had escaped to the West in the great exodus during the war. According to Osipov, she had then divorced him and remarried. In the course of time Osipov became involved with another woman, and, although by church law remarriage was strictly prohibited, in 1951 he married her in a civil ceremony (a simple procedure in which the couple merely registers with a state office as man and wife).

This, of course, scandalized the church. Remarriage was impossible for a priest, and thus in the church's eyes Osipov not only was living in open, adulterous cohabitation, but had publicly registered this insult to his church for the world to see. Normally such a priest would be subject to immediate excommunication. In Osipov's case he was allowed to continue his professorial duties, probably because he was virtually irreplaceable on the faculty at the Leningrad Academy, although one cannot discount the possibility that the state might conceivably have exerted pressure in his behalf.[2] He was prohibited, however, from celebrating the sacraments or continuing the vocational activities of the priesthood.

On December 6, 1959, Osipov defected. He renounced the Christian faith and publicly embraced atheism. The Soviet state was in the early stages of mounting a renewed antireligious campaign, and Osipov quickly became the stellar attraction of atheist propaganda, writing numerous articles against Christianity, and joining those ex-priests whose propaganda told of the grossest forms of clerical hypocrisy, avarice, peculation, licentiousness, and immorality of all sorts that they claimed to have witnessed during their years in the priesthood.[3]

According to Osipov, his reason for converting to atheism was an intellectual conviction that religion was untrue. Over a period of years doubts had gradually multiplied until he could no longer in good conscience continue his activities as a teacher of Old Testament. Indeed, his last years at the academy were inconsonant with his convictions, for he had become convinced beyond doubt that Christianity was totally false long before he publicly renounced the faith. Perhaps this is indeed what happened, and there were no reasons for Osipov's defection other than those he recounted in the pages of *Pravda*.[4] However, it would be wise to bear in mind that the Secret Police was notorious for its use of blackmail in breaking the resistance of its subjects, and the use of sexual compromise had a long and unhappy record in the history of the Soviet Secret Police.[5]

An incredible event happened on December 30, 1959. The Moscow patriarchate excommunicated Osipov and two other defectors to atheism.[6]

Osipov was being highly publicized in the Soviet press as an eminent example of a man of intellectual honesty, ideals, and courage of convictions. He was very much the major star of Soviet antireligious propaganda. To excommunicate such a favorite of the state would have been no idle decision on the patriarchate's part, for it amounted to a direct challenge, an affront to the Soviet regime. To the state's claims that Osipov was a hero, an example of Soviet manhood well worth emulation, the Russian Orthodox Church was replying that he was the most despicable of men, unworthy of the continued fellowship or even contact of Christian people.

The challenge was the more evident in view of the fact that four decades earlier the church's first response to the accession of the Communist Party to power in Russia was Patriarch Tikhon's excommunication of all Communists, which was the opening maneuver in a bitter attack on the new regime. Excommunication was still the most powerful weapon in the church's meager arsenal, and this was the first time since 1918 that it had been turned against the state.

Excommunication is an exceedingly serious matter in the Russian Orthodox Church. It cannot be pronounced by the patriarch alone, but must be enacted by the ruling synod of bishops acting in concert. The church knew its own history very well indeed, and it was fully aware of what excommunication of Communists had meant in the past. Osipov's condemnation, therefore, represented a studied measure applied by the church in full realization of the meaning of the action.

Nikolai, of course, as a leading bishop of the church, was a party to the action. In fact, the challenge to the state, which was implicit in the action, may have been undertaken, if not on his initiative, at least with his solid support. Nikolai, after all, was the cleric most intimately connected with the state, for he had borne the chief responsibility for church collaboration with the government. Because of his long experience, he would be the single bishop best able to predict what the reaction of the state would be, and thus his analysis would have been crucial in the considerations leading to the excommunication.

More importantly, Nikolai would probably be the chief recipient of the wrath of the state. It was he whose collaboration had been most prominent in the negotiated *détente* between church and state. His cooperation, which was expressive of that of the church, had been the price paid by the church in return for the concessions granted by the state. Now the church, in condemning Osipov, was breaking its part of the bargain by challenging the state.

The condemnation of Osipov was merely the beginning. Not content with challenging the state on this issue alone, the church made a series of moves in rapid succession that amounted almost to a full-scale attack against the Soviet regime. Nikolai took an exceedingly active role in this astounding confrontation, and was to be the chief focus of the state's wrath before the affair was over. It was almost as though Nikolai and the leadership of the Russian Orthodox Church had chosen to make a definite break with the habitual subservience to the regime.

On February 16 Patriarch Aleksii took part in a Conference of the Soviet Public for Disarmament in Moscow. At that conference Aleksii gave an oration the like of which had not been heard in Russia for forty years.[7] He began his talk with a ringing series of claims in praise of the great role the Russian Orthodox Church had played throughout Russian history. It was the church that had built, educated, and supported the Russian people. If this were so, then the obvious implication was that the greatness of the Russian people was not due to the Communist Party, but was attributable only to the Orthodox church. Aleksii's complete failure to mention the Soviet government in connection with the greatness of the Russian people was pointed. He turned his attention briefly to the church's activities in the Peace Campaign, making the minimum necessary mention of the government's support for peace. Then the Patriarch concluded his short oration with the resounding proclamation that the church had survived all kinds of human enmity throughout its history, that Christ had foretold the ultimate downfall of its foes, and that the gates of hell would not prevail against the church of Christ.

This brought the challenge into the open. The church had not taken such a stand as this since its resounding defeat in open struggle with the Communists in the year immediately following the Revolution, and for it to claim for itself the primary credit for the nation's greatness in the conditions of 1960 was an affront to the Communist regime. For these claims to be made by the head of the church himself amounted to open defiance by the church. For this defiance to be expressed at a secular conference convened by the state for the specific purpose of creating propaganda favorable to its foreign policy made the affront intolerable.

Nikolai was closely associated with this speech of the Patriarch's, and, to judge from the surface, it would seem that the state's response was to hold him personally responsible. At least one Western authority, a scholar of long and considerable experience in Russian Orthodoxy, felt that Nikolai may actually have written the speech delivered by Aleksii.[8] Whether this hypothesis be true or not, there is a striking similarity in content between Aleksii's speech in 1960 and Nikolai's sermon in New York in 1956. Nikolai, it will be recalled, had also described the magnificence of the role played by the Orthodox church in Russian history, and had predicted that thousands of years hence the church and its God would remain. This coincidence of theme is remarkable at the least, and may indicate that Nikolai's involvement in the Patriarch's action in 1960 was very intimate indeed.

On February 25, 1960, a ceremony was held honoring Patriarch Aleksii on his patron saint's day. The proceedings, as reported in the *Journal of the Moscow Patriarchate* (which was still under Nikolai's editorship) were incredible. According to that report, Nikolai greeted Aleksii with customary name-day salutations, referred to the recent fifteenth anniversary of his installation as patriarch, and continued:

In a brief [speech of] greeting it is impossible to enumerate what You, Your Holiness, have done during these fifteen years of Your patriarchate. You have strengthened the internal structure of our Church, You have raised the discipline of the clergy and laity. With Your blessing a series of theological books have been published. The establishment of active theological schools,

which was conceived by the late blessed Patriarch Sergii, has
been accomplished by You, and now many hundreds of young
pastors are laboring in the corn-field of Christ. You established
relations with the autocephalous Orthodox churches, which had
lapsed for thirty years before Your ascension to the throne, by
traveling Yourself to a number of Orthodox countries, by sending thither Your representatives to fortify the bonds of brotherhood, and by receiving the Patriarchs and representatives of
the Orthodox Churches to Yourself. You have seen that for the
past decade the Protestant world has been seeking to draw
closer to Orthodoxy, expressing deep interest in its spiritual
treasures, religious experience, and church order, and You have
blessed the invitation of Protestant delegations from many countries and have sent us to various countries in order to bear
witness there to Orthodoxy.

All know, the entire Christian and non-Christian world, Your
labors and Your services in the defense of peace: Your many
addresses, summonses, epistles, and blessings of Your representatives speaking for the Russian Orthodox Church at foreign
congresses and conferences.

In truth, what You have done these fifteen years is a great
feat!

We pray to the Lord God always, and today we pray, with
special vigor and devotion to You, that the Lord increase the
days of Your life and the days of Your patriarchate, and that
the Providence of God remove all grief from the Russian
Orthodox Church, that never and by no means may the labors
of our Church in the glory and salvation of the Orthodox believing people be diminished.

In the name of the Holy Synod, the episcopate, the theological schools, the monks, clerics, in the name of the believing
people gathered here, and—I take on myself the audacity to
say it—in the name of the entire believing Russian Orthodox
people, of all our Russian Orthodox church, with filial, fiery
devotion and joy I greet You, Your Holiness. . . .[9]

In his reply of thanks the Patriarch included the following statement:

In greeting you, our beloved archpastors, pastors, and flock, with these festivities of the Moscow Church, I express the hope that we all will be worthy of the prayers and protection of Saint Aleksii, by our life, our diligence, our faith, and our patience in bearing those unavoidable griefs which are rushing over us, over the Church of God, for the Lord Himself said: "In the world you shall have tribulation." We believe in the divine word of our Lord: "But believe, for I have overcome the world," that is, Christ has overcome all the insidious actions of the enemies of the Church, the enemies of God, and gives us the power to bear every grief which is unavoidable in this world. We believe that the Lord, according to the prayers of our protector, Saint Aleksii, Metropolitan of Moscow, will henceforth help us to overcome all difficulties and will give to us His blessing in the service of the Church of Christ henceforth.[10]

This was a truly astounding performance. The speech of Nikolai and the answer of Aleksii certainly were not extemporaneously delivered without regard to their significance. Not only do the two speeches seem almost like a well-rehearsed dialogue, an exchange of memorized speeches, their contents are so precisely complementary that they must have been worked out in advance. Beyond doubt, Nikolai and Aleksii had carefully planned the speeches together, and it is even possible that both speeches were written by one of them. For nobody in the Russian church would have made such statements as these without carefully considering them first.

It is noteworthy that in neither address was there any reference whatsoever to the Soviet government. This was a shocking departure from precedent, for it had long been

an unbreakable tradition that the beneficence of the Soviet
government would be praised somewhere in the course of
major church addresses. Particularly on such an occasion as
this, which celebrated both Aleksii's name-day and his fifteenth anniversary as patriarch, it was a decided affront to
neglect the customary ritual of praise to the government.

To make matters worse, Nikolai had specifically enumer-
ated the major achievements of the church, both within
Russia and abroad, and had ascribed exclusive credit for
them to the head of the church. It was unheard of to speak
of such things without giving the major share of the credit
to the Soviet government. Furthermore, many of the activities had been undertaken, if not at the specific demand of
the state, at least with its enthusiastic help and cooperation,
and were primarily designed to further its ends. Nikolai's
pointed exclusion of the state could only mean that the
church had decided to take full and exclusive credit for all
its successes. This amounted to nothing less than a repudiation of the entire concept of political cooperation with and
service to the state, which had been the accepted role of the
church for the preceding fifteen years.

Aleksii's reference to the enemies of the church and of
God was a stinging rebuke, for in Soviet conditions this
could only refer to the Communists. And Nikolai's reference to the "believing Russian Orthodox people" could
easily be interpreted as a direct attack against the Communists, implying that communism was a usurper and had
no right to be in Russia—the Russian people are the "believing Russian Orthodox people."

The reference to "grief," introduced by Nikolai and
elaborated on by Aleksii, was a general reference to the ris-
ing antireligious campaign, referring specifically to the
slanderous propaganda attacks, and perhaps foreseeing the

more active measures against the churches, which would surely come as the campaign continued its crescendo. More concretely, it indicated a full awareness that the actions taken by the patriarchate in resistance to the regime would receive an answer from the state, and this answer would not be pleasant for the church.

Aleksii's statement that Christ had overcome the world and his prayer that the church be enabled to overcome all difficulties was a direct challenge to the state, a pointed refutation of the Marxist doctrine, which the antireligious campaign was trying to fulfill, that the church must ultimately disappear entirely.

It was a bitter performance, a challenge so thoroughly and so obviously filled with hostility to the Communist regime that it could not have been ignored by the state. Coming as it did, as the climax to a series of deliberate provocations engineered by the church in what could only be interpreted as a repudiation of its accepted role of subservience to state policy, it made reaction by the state inevitable.

In fact, the state's response to the church's challenge had already begun. On February 21 *Izvestiia* had announced that Georgii G. Karpov, chairman of the Council for the Affairs of the Russian Orthodox Church, had been replaced by one Vladimir Kuroedov. Karpov, despite his rather unsavory background, had been relatively congenial to the church, and his replacement could not be a favorable portent. More importantly, Karpov, who had been the chief official contact between the church and state from 1943 to 1960, was associated in the public mind with the policy of limited accommodation to the needs of the church, which had been instituted by Stalin during the war. His removal might signify the end of the long pause in the regime's struggle against religion.

Kuroedov was a rather mysterious figure. Little is known of his background beyond a rather vague association with the Party apparatus. His appointment as chairman of the council was widely (and, as subsequent events were to prove, correctly) interpreted as signifying a harsher attitude toward the church on the part of the Soviet regime.[11]

The focus of the regime's response to the challenge of the church was Metropolitan Nikolai. He virtually disappeared from public view after February 1960. A quiet but futile struggle was waged in the monthly *Journal of the Moscow Patriarchate* during the spring of that year.[12] The March issue contained a long article praising Nikolai's work in the PEACE CAMPAIGN. The May and June issues, which normally carried each year's Easter greetings received by the church from abroad, devoted only two pages to greetings addressed to Patriarch Aleksii, but eighteen pages to those received by Metropolitan Nikolai. Apparently the journal was doing its best to buttress Nikolai's position by giving maximum publicity to the respect and affection commanded by Nikolai in the outside world, in the hope that realization of the power of his contacts outside of Russia would prevent state action against him. The journal appeared to be trying to demonstrate to the state that Nikolai was too powerful a figure to interfere with, that contemplation of his removal from office would involve great risks for the Soviet government's image abroad.

We do not know what Nikolai's reactions during this period were. Indeed, we know very little about his activities, let alone what his own attitude may have been. His career and perhaps his very life were in serious jeopardy as a result of the stand he and the church had taken against the government, and the events of the spring of 1960 constituted the final, critical struggle of his entire public life. On April 5 a publicity stunt was held in Moscow in support of the Soviet campaign to discredit the West German government. Dr. Theodor Oberlaender, the West German Minister for Refugees, was indicted *in absentia* as a Nazi war criminal. The trial was under the auspices of the old Extraordinary State Commission, of which Nikolai had been a charter member. According to a reporter of *The New York Times*, Nikolai was present at the trial. We are not told what role, if any, he played in the proceedings.[13]

At the end of April Michael Bourdeaux, a young Anglican studying at the Moscow State University under the cultural exchange program, was invited for a brief interview with Nikolai. He had applied for this interview some eight months previously through a letter from the Archbishop of York. Why this exceedingly critical time in Nikolai's career was chosen to grant the request is not known. The following is Bourdeaux's account of the meeting:

He was undoubtedly a busy man at the time, but even so I had not expected that my reception would be so extremely brief. He treated me as if I were an official delegation from the Anglican Church, asking me about the state of health of some of its most prominent members, inquiring whether Dr. Hewlett Johnson were still alive, whether the Archbishop of Canterbury intended to retire and who was the Bishop of London. He went on to ask me a few personal questions about what I was doing in Russia, what my plans for the future were and whether I was married. When I told him I was to be ordained later in the year and that I was engaged to be married, he spent the rest of the time asking about my fiancee and requesting me to pass on his best wishes to her. All this was very pleasant, but of no practical use to me at all. In fact during the whole of the five minutes which I spent in his company, he did not give me the chance to ask a single question; when I thought he had finished the introductory part of the interview and was wondering

which question to ask him first, he stood up to signify that the
end of my time had come.[14]

In ordinary circumstances the interview would have been
a normal courtesy on Nikolai's part, without further significance. However, considering the extreme jeopardy in
which Nikolai's career lay at the time, one may wonder
whether more than ordinary courtesy lay behind Nikolai's
granting of the interview.

The initial questions concerning leaders of the Church of
England do not seem inconsistent with an exceedingly
cautious attempt to probe whether the interview might not
be used in eliciting from the West some expression of support for Nikolai, support that was desperately needed if his
career were to be salvaged. Unfortunately, neither Bourdeaux nor the Christian leadership of the West was at all
aware of the hidden struggle taking place behind the scenes
in Nikolai's life. If this was actually Nikolai's purpose in
granting the interview, he quickly was able to discern this
lack of awareness, and apparently concluded that the young
student whom fortune had presented to him at this critical
hour could not be of help.

On the other hand, it is possible that the granting of the
interview was prompted by exactly opposite reasoning.
Perhaps the state, then in the process of forcing the end of
Nikolai's career, had had its attention drawn to the all but
forgotten letter from the Archbishop of York, and had
feared the outside possibility that if this request were ignored
attention might be drawn to Nikolai and interfere with the
state's plans for his removal. Thus the state might have considered it expedient for Nikolai to grant a token interview.

In either case (and they are not mutually exclusive),
Nikolai would be under exceedingly close covert supervision during the interview, so it is not surprising that the

young student, unaware as he was of the drama taking place behind the scenes, found the interview so disappointing.

On May 18 a curious speech appeared over Nikolai's signature. The U-2 scandal had broken, Khrushchev had canceled the Paris summit meeting, and a Meeting of Soviet Public Opinion was convened to propagandize the affair. One of the speeches at this gathering was attributed to Nikolai by the *Journal of the Moscow Patriarchate*.

For such a long time world public opinion has striven for a meeting of the great powers, and it did not come to pass by the fault of the U.S.A.! How can the leaders of the U.S.A. not be conscious of general responsibility for the fate of peace?!

We, people of various callings, occupations, and professions, have gathered here today in order to share our experiences and hopes. Peace! Cooperation! The necessity of a meeting at the highest level! The requirements to the U.S.A. for agreement to the bases for the convocation of that meeting, which were justly expressed in the last statement of N. S. Khrushchev, who has made such a huge contribution in the matter of peace—this is the main content of our experiences and hopes. And we know why we express them in one and the same words: all people dream of the bright day of boundless life, and freedom from fear of war is dear to each of us!

Do not all peoples of the earth have that same experience in these days? Do not they remember the terrible sufferings experienced a decade and a half ago? Do they not listen with horror and indignation to talk of the terrible consequences of the recent nuclear bomb tests? Are not they agitated, as we are, at the outrageous provocations of American reactionary circles?

. . . Together with all our peace loving people we express indignation at the latest shameless provocation by aircraft and by the statements of American leaders which led to the impossibility of carrying out the long awaited meeting. We fully support the statement of N. S. Khrushchev in Paris on the in-

famous conduct of the government of the U.S.A. in relations
with the Soviet Union! This statement was an absolutely necessary expression of the dignity of our country, our people.

    . . . It is difficult even to think that the leaders of Christian
countries, which had gathered to carry out the conference, did
not condemn the acts of aggression which were fully known to
us, as expressions of an ideology which is inimical to Christianity. How shameful this is for them![15]

It had been years since Nikolai had delivered anything
like this speech. Perhaps its content should not be surprising,
for many, many people, both in Russia and abroad, thought
this was probably a matter for very vigorous criticism. Such
criticism might imply a relatively unsophisticated view of
international relations, an ignorance of the uncomfortable
fact that clandestine information-gathering has always existed. Therefore, intelligent criticism of the U-2 affair would
more properly be concerned with how the affair was handled rather than with the existence of the flights themselves.
But in all fairness, Nikolai could unquestionably have made
a good case for his position.

The more startling dimension of this speech was its tone,
for not since 1956 had Nikolai's utterances been so highly
colored with propagandistic polemic. The outspokenness,
the unrestrained vocabulary and phrasing, and the general
acerbity of the attack contrast markedly with his statements
of the preceding four years. Compared with the delicate
finesse of his statement regarding Hungary, for example, or
with the careful, balanced references to yet unsettled problems in his remarks regarding the World Council of
Churches in 1958, the change of tone seems curious indeed.

Inasmuch as this speech of May 18, 1960, contrasts so
markedly with Nikolai's speeches during the preceding three
years or more, there must always remain the possibility that

this speech was not written by Nikolai. It could possibly have been written by state propagandists and then fraudulently ascribed to Nikolai, or delivered by him under duress. Aside from its immediate usefulness in the U-2 issue it is possible that the state might have conceived of such a speech in order that possible foreign protests might be averted when Nikolai was deposed and stripped of his ecclesiastical position. It might have been hoped that this reversion to rank propagandism might have reinforced Western Christianity's suspicion of Nikolai, and hence would have discouraged any protest about his disappearance.

If, as seems more likely, Nikolai did indeed give the speech as claimed, it might indicate considerable inner doubt and confusion on Nikolai's part. Perhaps he realized the dire consequences of resistance to the state; perhaps he was attempting by this speech to recant, to demonstrate a renewed willingness to collaborate with the state. Certainly the *Journal's* publication of the speech might indicate that the Orthodox church was having second thoughts about its abortive resistance to the state, and might have been evidence of an almost desperate desire to return to the old pattern of church-state relations, which the church had repudiated only three months earlier.

The wrath of the state was not to be averted, however, especially not insofar as Nikolai was concerned. He had been prominently absent from the Easter services.[16] His political disgrace was evident in his absence from PEACE CAMPAIGN activities. On June 21 the Holy Synod of the Church decided to grant by decree "the request of His Eminence, Metropolitan of Krutitskii and Kolomna Nikolai, for his release from the duties of Chairman of the Department of External Church relations of the Moscow Patriarchate."[17]

Three months later (the delay may have been designed to

give the state time to moderate its designs against Nikolai
in response to protest by Western church leaders in support
of Nikolai; no such protest was forthcoming), on September 19, 1960, the Synod decreed the "release [of the] Metropolitan of Krutitskii and Kolomna Nikolai, in accordance
with his request of September 15 of this year, from the duties
of Metropolitan of Krutitskii and Kolomna."[18]

Nikolai's career was over. One may doubt the sincerity
of Nikolai's requests that he be discarded, if such requests
were ever given at all by Nikolai. That the hand of the state
was behind the decision to depose him was obvious to all. It
is quite unthinkable—practically unheard of in the history
of the modern Russian church—for an Orthodox bishop to
be removed from the episcopate for reasons other than
health.[19] And no question of health appeared in either decree
of the Holy Synod.

Almost immediately, rumors of Nikolai's death began to
circulate.[20] That some of these rumors were brought to the
West by visiting representatives of the Moscow patriarchate
as early as summer and fall of 1960 probably indicates that
Nikolai had disappeared entirely and not even the church
knew what the state had done with him, although there is a
possibility that the rumors were circulated with state con-
nivance in order to gauge Western reaction to the idea of his
eventual death.

Actually, Nikolai did not die until December 13, 1961,
almost two years to the day from the defection of Osipov,
and precisely one week after the conclusion of the New
Delhi Conference of the World Council of Churches. It was
extraordinarily fortunate for the state's public image that
Nikolai remained alive until then, for it was at the New
Delhi Conference that the Russian Orthodox Church was
admitted into membership in the World Council of

Churches, bringing to successful conclusion the negotiations that had begun almost four years earlier while Nikolai was still spokesman for the church's foreign affairs. Had Nikolai died before he did, it is not unthinkable that the curious end to his career might have elicited sufficient reaction in the West to frustrate the negotiations.

Nikolai's death was ostensibly of heart failure. Shortly before his death a Western visitor asked for an interview with him and was told that he had been hospitalized. The hospitalization, it was implied, was necessitated because of Nikolai's recent practice of taking too many medicines.

There were exceedingly strange circumstances surrounding his death.

According to a letter sent from Russia, he was kept in absolute isolation, and not even his sister, a Russian Orthodox nun, was allowed to see him during his terminal illness, although she made repeated attempts during the week before his death. His body, according to the letter, was treated with utter indifference, if not contempt, at the morgue.[21] Almost immediately, rumors of murder arose, and these rumors have persisted, both in the West and in Russia.[22]

At Nikolai's funeral, attended by exceedingly large crowds at the monastery of Zagorsk, near Moscow, members of a group of Western churchmen were told by people there that no funeral would have been held at all except for the insistence of the large crowds that appeared at Zagorsk and would not be put off.[23] Nikolai was buried in utter disgrace, so far as the state was concerned. There was no mention of his death in the newspapers, although it is customary for state papers to give obituary notice and eulogies on the death of prominent citizens. The fact that Nikolai was the recipient of two state medals (the Defense of Moscow medal and the Red Banner of Labor awarded him in

1955 for his peace activities) and no less than seven honorary doctorates (from eastern European universities and the Moscow Theological Academy) confirms the fact that the silence of state newspapers was a studied insult.

It was a large and deeply sorrowing crowd that witnessed Nikolai's funeral. Nikolai had become a great hero of the faith in the believers' eyes, and more so because of the heroism they saw in his final resistance to the state and his expulsion by the state. To many of those present his death was a martyr's death. To them it seemed the supreme act of heathen bestiality committed by a godless state. Perhaps this popular reaction to Nikolai's death explains the somewhat peculiar tone of Patriarch Aleksii's eulogy of the sixty-eight-year-old Nikolai:

. . . We should not judge whether a man's life ends timely or untimely. For the Lord sets the limits of a man's life, and no one can extend or diminish the years of his life. All is determined by the Lord God, and therefore we, remaining here on earth and leading those dear to him in all their earthly path, should be comforted that the Lord, according to His love for the departed, has received the soul of our beloved brother.[24]

The Patriarch's last sentence in that statement merely echoed a phrase in the Russian Orthodox litany for the dead: "Though he sinned, yet he did not depart from Thee."[25]

Notes

I. INTRODUCTION

1. See: John Shelton Curtiss, *The Russian Church and the Soviet State, 1917–1950* (Boston: Little, Brown, and Company, 1953); Stanley George Evans, *The Russian Church To-day* (London: Zeno Publishers, 1955); Walter Kolarz, *Religion in the Soviet Union* (New York: St. Martin's Press, 1962); Orthodox Eastern Church, Russian, *The Russian Orthodox Church, Organization, Situation, Activity* (Moscow: The Patriarchate, 1959); and Nikita Struve, *Les Chrétiens en U.R.S.S.* (Paris: Editions du Seuil, 1963).

2. See: Donald A. Lowrie, "Children's Crusade in Reverse," *Christian Century*, September 16, 1964, pp. 1141–42; Nadezhda Teodorovich, "Increasing Pressure on the Moscow Patriarchate," *Bulletin of the Institute for the Study of the USSR*, October 1962, pp. 46–47. Cf. *Kommunist*, August 1959. There was a gradual increase in antireligious propaganda prior to the Central Committee of the Communist Party of the Soviet Union's order of January 10, 1960, for greater efforts in this field (see A. Hakimoglu, "Forty Years of Anti-Religious Propaganda," *East Turkic Review*, December 1960, p. 69).

3. Some 800,000 members of the Society for the Dissemination of Scientific and Political Knowledge could be mobilized to the task (*Pravda*, April 3, 1959, and January 27, 1960), and distribution points had been established in many cities and towns (Kolarz, *op. cit.*, p. 18).

4. See: V. S. Ovchinnikov, "The Foundations of Scientific Atheism in the Technical Schools," *Voprosy Filosofii*, July 1961, pp. 141–44, translation in *Joint Publications Research Service*

(*JPRS*) 11798, "Translations on Religion in the USSR," No. 7, December 29, 1961, pp. 1–8. Two universities of atheism had been established (T. Otto Nall, "The Hope for Religion in Russia," *Christian Century*, April 4, 1959, p. 262), and in his famous endorsement of the antireligious campaign, Il'ichev, the chairman of the Ideological Commission of the Party's Central Committee urged that their number be multiplied (*Partiinaia Zhizn'*, February 1964, pp. 22–26; cf. *Kommunist*, September 23, 1964). Local schools of atheism were established in many areas (*Partiinaia Zhizn'*, March 1965, p. 80; *Sovetskaia Kirgiziia*, October 10, 1964).

5. See: *Sovety Deputatov Trudiashchikhsia*, October 1960, pp. 19–26; *Pravda*, June 7, 1964; E. Lisavtsev, "New rites—in the life of the people!" *Sovetskie Profsoiuzy*, January 1965, p. 33; V. Zelenchuk, *et al.*, "New life—new holidays and rites," *Kommunist Moldavii*, February 1965, pp. 22–26; *Zaria Vostoka*, August 29, 1964; and *Kommunist Tadzhikistana*, August 2, 1964. These rites repeated experiments of the thirties, which had been conspicuous for their lack of success; see, e.g.: *Antireligioznik*, August 1937, p. 44, and August 1939, p. 44; Kolarz, *op. cit.*, p. 33.

6. See: *Komsomol'skaia Pravda*, August 31, 1962; A. Baigushev, "Day against Night," *Literature i Zhizn'*, April 9, 1961, p. 2, translation in *Current Digest of the Soviet Press* (CDSP), May 24, 1961, pp. 14–15. Considerable efforts were also devoted to the production of antireligious motion pictures (*ibid.*; I. Kichanova, "Inadequacies of Atheism Courses in Higher Education," *Komsomol'skaia Pravda*, August 31, 1962, p. 3, translation in *CDSP*, September 26, 1962, pp. 17–18).

7. See: *Kommunist Belorussii*, September 1964, p. 54; *Pravda*, September 26, 1962, translation in *Religion in Communist Dominated Areas* (RCDA), November 5, 1962, p. 3; E. F. Murav'ev and Iu. V. Dmitriev, "Concreteness in Studying and Overcoming Religious Survivals," *Voprosy Filosofii*, March 1961, pp. 63–73, translations in *Soviet Review*, July 1961, p. 64 and *CDSP*, June 14, 1961, pp. 3–7; F. Kalita, "Atheists on the Offensive," *Pravda*, October 7, 1963, translated excerpts in *RCDA*, December 23, 1963, pp. 247–48; Stephen S. Rosenfeld, "Faith Is Evident in Russia Despite Persecutions," Washington *Post*, August 14, 1962; and *Sovety Deputatov Trudiashchikhsia*, *loc. cit.* The potential of this approach had long been recognized but never systematically exploited (cf. B. V., "From Experience of Work Among Believers," *Antireligioznik*, October–November 1940, p. 70; E. Iaroslavskii, "The Next Tasks of the Antireligious Front," *Pravda*, June 15, 1929, p. 5). A similar unexplored field, which was given new

emphasis in the sixties, was psychology of religion (Richard H. Marshall, Jr., "A New Dimension in Scientific Atheism," *Catholic World*, July 1964, pp. 239-42; cf. *Pod Znamenem Marksizma*, March–April 1933, pp. 278-79).

8. See: speech by first secretary of the Central Committee of the Belorussian Communist Party on February 17, 1960, quoted by Yury Marin, "The Search for New Methods in the Fight against Religion," in Boris Iwanow, ed., *Religion in the USSR* (Munich: Institute for the Study of the USSR, 1960), p. 215; speech by first secretary of the Central Committee of the Moldavian Communist Party on January 28, 1960, quoted by Marin, *ibid.*, p. 214; and E. Rozenbaum, "Decree on Freedom of Conscience," *Nauka i Religiia*, March 1963, pp. 35-48, translation in *RCDA*, June 17, 1963, pp. 109-11. The bulk of these laws were first promulgated in 1929 (P. V. Gidulianov, *Otdelenie Tserkvi ot Gosudarstva (Separation of Church from State)* [Moscow: State Publishing House for Juridical Literature, 1929], p. 225).

9. Article 227 of the Criminal Code of the R.S.F.S.R. prescribes a sentence of three to five years' deprivation of freedom for religious activity that is "harmful to health," "prompts citizens to nonparticipation in social activity or nonfulfillment of civil duties," or that entices minors into the group (*Ugolovnyi Kodeks RSFSR (Criminal Code of the RSFSR)* [Moscow: "Juridical Literature" Press, 1964], p. 91).

10. T. E. Bird, "Party, the Patriarch, and the World Council," *Commonweal*, April 13, 1962, p. 55. A second change in emphasis occurred with the publication of the rule that it was this body that was to give final permission for the closing of churches (A. Valentinov, "Soviet Legislation on Cults," *Nauka i Religiia*, October 1961, p. 92, translation in *JPRS* 11797, "Translations on Religion in the USSR," No. 8, December 29, 1961, pp. 44-51).

11. *Zhurnal Moskovskoi Patriarkhii*, August 1961, p. 6.

12. Cf. the Central Committee's order of January 10, 1960 (above). It was reported that at the Twenty-first Party Congress in 1960 a secret resolution was adopted urging the elimination of all religion within the next Seven-Year Plan (Donald A. Lowrie, "Russian Church at New Delhi," *Christian Century*, November 1, 1961, p. 1299). The Society for the Dissemination of Scientific and Political Knowledge, which had sole responsibility for antireligious propaganda, held a congress in January 1960, attended by many of the highest figures of the regime, including Kosygin, Brezhnev, Mikoyan, Suslov, Ignatev, and Polyansky (*Pravda*, January 27, 1960). Orders were given to regional Party organizations for strict enforce-

ment of all laws relating to religious organizations (*Sovetskaia Belorussiia*, February 18, 1960; *Sovetskaia Moldaviia*, January 29, 1960). In 1961 Khrushchev himself called for greater efforts against religion in his address to the Twenty-second Congress (*Pravda*, October 18, 1961), and Il'ichev repeated the call at a closed session in 1963 (*Bakinski Rabochii*, June 19, 1963, translation in *RCDA*, August 19, 1963, p. 152). In January 1964 Il'ichev, in the name of the Central Committee, published a fourteen-point order for a vastly increased antireligious campaign (*Partiinaia Zhizn*,' February 1964, p. 22–26).

13. These procedures included denial of building materials for necessary repairs (Valentinov, *loc. cit.*), closing of local shrines because of technicalities (*Sovety Deputatov Trudiashchikhsia, loc. cit.*), forbidding professional singers from church choirs (Johann von Gardner, "The State of Orthodox Church Music in the USSR," *Bulletin of the Institute for the Study of the USSR*, April 1963, p. 10), and stationing of peoples policemen at church doors (*Uchitel'skaia Gazeta*, November 30, 1963) and formation of patrols of Young Communists to follow people who attend church (*Leninskaia Smena*, September 20, 1959), both of which were obviously designed to discourage church attendance.

14. This measure was first applied against Baptists (*Slavic Gospel News Bulletin*, June 1962, p. 9; W. C. Fletcher, "Soviet Society and Religion: A Trip Report," *Communist Affairs*, June–August 1963, p. 11). Late in 1963 the prohibition was extended to Orthodox as well, according to the testimony of Paul B. Anderson (U.S. Congress, House, Committee on Foreign Affairs, *Recent Developments in the Soviet Bloc* [Washington D.C.: U.S. Government Printing Office, 1964], p. 101).

15. See: Academy of Sciences of the USSR, *Uspekhi Sovremennoi Nauki i Religiia* (*Contemporary Science's Success and Religion*) (Moscow: Academy Press, 1961), p. 26; Donald A. Lowrie, "Eastern Christians under Duress," *Christian Century*, November 21, 1962, p. 1424; and Fletcher, *loc. cit.* This complete prohibition of the right to catechize was a more severe restriction than those applied in the thirties, when priests were allowed to teach the catechism only at the invitation of parents and in groups not exceeding three members (Gidulianov, *loc. cit.*). There was also an almost universal application of the 1935 practice of requiring the consent of both parents prior to the baptism of an infant, even though no such law was officially extant (*Nauka i Religiia*, April 1964, pp. 83–85; *New Statesman*, May 2, 1959, p. 596).

16. See: *Sel'skaia Zhizn'*, June 14, 1962, and June 20, 1962; *Izvestiia*, June 28, 1962; *Kazakhstanskaia Pravda*, June 24, 1964; *Voiov-*

nychy Ateist, January 1962, p. 14, and February 1962, p. 19; *Turkmenskaia Iskra,* September 1962, translations in *Survey of the Soviet Press,* October 29, 1962, and *RCDA,* March 18, 1963, pp. 11–13; *Pravda,* October 3, 1964, p. 4, translation in *CDSP,* October 28, 1964, p. 32; D. Konstantinov, "Further Blows at Religion," *Bulletin of the Institute for the Study of the USSR,* November 1962, p. 53; and Harry Willetts, "Deopiating the Masses," *Problems of Communism,* November–December 1964, p. 37. Cf. F. Agafonov, "Without Proper Sharpness, Aggressiveness," *Kommunist Belorusii,* February 1966, p. 68. These cases were confirmed by the thirty-two Christians from Siberia who sought asylum at the American Embassy in Moscow in January 1963. Among the documents they left at the Embassy were several letters written from state boarding schools (*Newsweek,* January 14, 1963, p. 32 and January 28, 1963, pp. 45–46; George Bailey, "Religion in the Soviet Union," *The Reporter,* July 16, 1964, p. 28). The severity of such denial of parental rights was without precedent in Soviet history (cf. E. Iaroslavskii, *O Religii* (*On Religion*) [Moscow: State Publishing House for Political Literature, 1957], p. 186). Denial of parental rights was given ideological basis in 1962 at a Young Communist Congress, when it was explained that freedom of conscience does not apply to children, and no parent should be allowed spiritually to cripple a child (*Izvestiia,* April 17, 1962). Formal and legal basis was supplied in an article in an authoritative legal periodical, which explained that the state, because it grants parental rights, has the power to withdraw them, in some cases even before a case has been brought to the courts (*Sovetskaia Iustitsiia,* No. 21, 1962, translation in *Soviet Law and Government,* Spring 1963, pp. 46–47). A local ruling of 1964 stipulated that parents who have been deprived of parental rights must continue to provide for the support of the children (*Kazakhstanskaia Pravda,* June 24, 1964).

17. In 1961 an antireligious article noted that five hundred churches had been closed in two provinces alone (*Komsomol'skaia Pravda,* June 14, 1961). When it joined the World Council of Churches in 1961, Russian Orthodoxy claimed to have twenty thousand churches. This figure was probably inflated, for Soviet antireligious propaganda has indicated that the maximum number of churches operating in the postwar period was "more than fifteen thousand" (A. Veshchikov, "Milestones of a Great Journey," *Nauka i Religiia,* November 1962, p. 60, translation in *RCDA,* December 24, 1962, p. 8).

18. N. I. Yudin, *Pravda o Petersburgskikh "Sviatyniakh"* (*The Truth about the "Shrines" of St. Petersburg*) (Leningrad:

Lenin Press, 1962), translation in *RCDA*, June 24, 1963, p. 117. This figure was apparently confirmed by representatives of the church (testimony of Paul B. Anderson in U.S. House, Committee on Foreign Affairs, *op. cit.*, p. 99).

19. *Commonweal*, November 15, 1963, p. 211.

20. See: *France-Soir*, March 19, 1964, p. 5; London *Times*, January 4, 1965, p. 9; and David Floyd, "Russia's Religious Revival," London *Telegraph*, December 22, 1964. Cf. "Statement of Byelo-Russian Clergy and Laity," *One Church*, September–December 1964, pp. 188–90; Comité d'Information sur la Situation des Chrétiens en Union Soviétique, *Situation des Chrétiens en Union Soviétique* (Paris: n.p., 1965), II, *passim*.

21. London *Times, loc. cit.*

22. See: Teodorovich, *loc. cit.*, pp. 43, 46; American Committee for Liberation, *The Beleaguered Fortress* (New York: Information Center on Soviet Affairs, 1963), p. 14; "The Russian Orthodox Church and the Soviet Leadership," *Soviet Affairs Analysis Service*, No. 17, 1961–62, p. 7; and Constantin de Grunwald, *The Churches and the Soviet Union* (New York: The Macmillan Company, 1962), pp. 95–96. Many more high prelates came under propaganda attack (N. Teodorovich, "The Episcopacy and Diocesan Network of the Moscow Patriarchate," *Bulletin of the Institute for the Study of the USSR*, June 1961, p. 52).

23. Michael Bourdeaux, *Opium of the People* (London: Faber and Faber, Ltd., 1965), p. 212; cf. *Slavic Gospel News Bulletin*, January–March 1962, p. 11.

24. For the *modus vivendi* between church and state prior to 1960 see William C. Fletcher, *A Study in Survival* (New York: The Macmillan Company, 1965), *passim*.

25. For biographical data on Nikodim see: Bourdeaux, *op. cit.*, pp. 221–23; Dmitrii Konstantinov, "The Orthodox Church, the Regime, and the People Today," *Bulletin of the Institute for the Study of the USSR*, February 1962, pp. 49–50; Yury Marin, "The Moscow Patriarchate in Soviet Foreign Policy," *ibid.*, February 1961, p. 34; Dmitrii Konstantinov, "A Turning Point in the Moscow Patriarchate's Policy," *ibid.*, March 1963, p. 26; I. Swan, "The Disappearance of Metropolitan Nikolai," *ibid.*, May 1961, pp. 47–48; Bird, *loc. cit.*, p. 56; *Time*, January 6, 1961; *New Statesman*, November 24, 1961; and Lorie, "Russian Church at New Delhi," *loc. cit.*

26. Biographical data on Sergii are from Wassilij Alexeev, *The Foreign Policy of the Moscow Patriarchate, 1939–1953* (New York: Research Program on the USSR, 1953), pp. 65–99, and from his article, "Death of Exarch Sergii Voskresenskii and Election of the Moscow Patriarch According to Secret Ger-

man Documents," which was generously supplied to me by the author.

II. YEARS OF BACKGROUND

1. V. Nikonov, "His Grace Nikolai, Metropolitan of Krutitskii and Kolomna," *Zhurnal Moskovskoi Patriarkhii*, April 1952, p. 12.
2. Wassilij Alexeev, *The Foreign Policy of the Moscow Patriarchate, 1939–1953* (New York: Research Program on the USSR, 1953), p. 103.
3. Nikonov, *loc. cit.*, p. 13.
4. For events in the history of the Russian church from 1917–1943 see William C. Fletcher, *A Study in Survival* (New York: The Macmillan Company, 1965).
5. Alexeev, *op. cit.*, p. 105.
6. See Simon Wolin and Robert M. Slusser, eds., *The Soviet Secret Police* (New York: Frederick A. Praeger, Inc., 1957). Pages 355–68 contain an extensive bibliography, to which the many similar works published by the U.S. Government Printing Office for various Congressional bodies should be added.
7. Mikhail Pol'skii, *Kanonicheskoe Polozhenie Vysshei Tserkovnoi Vlasti v S.S.S.R. i Zagranitsei* (*The Canonical Position of the Highest Church Authority in the USSR and Abroad*) (Jordanville, N.Y.: Iov Pochaevskii Press in the Holy Trinity Monastery, 1948), pp. 99–100.
8. See Fletcher, *op. cit.*, pp. 92, 149.
9. *Izvestiia*, August 18, 1927, p. 3.
10. Nikonov, *loc. cit.*, p. 17.
11. See, e.g., Pol'skii, *op. cit.*, *passim*.

III. WAR

1. Nikita Struve, *Les Chrétiéns en U.R.S.S.* (Paris: Editions du Seuil, 1963), p. 55.
2. For the Battle of Moscow see: Alexander Werth, *Russia at War, 1941–1945* (New York: E. P. Dutton & Co., Inc., 1964); Herbert S. Dinerstein and Leon Gouré, *Two Studies in Soviet Controls* (Glencoe, Ill.: Free Press of Glencoe, 1955).
3. See William C. Fletcher, *A Study in Survival* (New York: The Macmillan Company, 1965), pp. 102–7.
4. *Zhurnal Moskovskoi Patriarkhii* (*Journal of the Moscow Patriarchate*, hereafter cited as *ZMP*), October 1944 (reprinted in Nikolai, Metropolitan of Kolomna, *Slova, Rechi, Poslaniia, 1941–1946* gg. [*Words, Speeches, Epistles, 1941–1946*, hereafter cited as *Slova* . . .] [Moscow: The Patriarchate, 1947], p. 198).
5. Orthodox Eastern Church, Russia, *The Truth about Religion in*

Russia, authorized translation by E. N. C. Sergeant of *Pravda o Religii v Rossiia* (New York: Hutchinson, 1944), p. 105.

6. *Ibid.,* p. 52.

7. USSR, *Soviet War Documents* (Washington, D.C.: Embassy of the USSR, 1943), p. 157.

8. See Fletcher, *loc. cit.*

9. *Pravda o Religii v Rossiia* (Moscow: The Patriarchate, 1942).

10. Included in his *We Will Defend Peace!* (Moscow: The Patriarchate, 1952).

11. Thaddeus Wittlin, *Time Stopped at 6:30* (New York: The Bobbs-Merrill Co., Inc., 1965), gives a convenient, if somewhat journalistic, account of the evidence.

12. Orthodox Eastern Church, Russian, *Pravda o Religii v Rossiia,* p. 216.

13. *Ibid.*

14. For the church's wartime assistance to the state see Fletcher, *op. cit.,* pp. 109–12.

15. *Slova . . .,* pp. 184–86.

16. ZMP, April 1944 (*Slova . . .,* pp. 191–92).

17. *Izvestiia,* September 5, 1943.

18. For the concordat and council of 1943 see Fletcher, *op. cit.,* pp. 112–15. The proceedings of the council may be found in Orthodox Eastern Church, Russian, *Patriarkh Sergii i Ego Dukhovnoe Nasledstsvo (Patriarch Sergii and His Spiritual Legacy)* (Moscow: The Patriarchate, 1947).

19. For the relationship of the Council for the Affairs of the Russian Orthodox Church to the Secret Police see Simon Wolin and Robert M. Slusser, eds., *The Soviet Secret Police* (New York: Frederick A. Praeger, Inc., 1957), pp. 23–24, 123, 330–31, 381.

20. *Ibid.,* p. 23.

21. For Nikolai's role in the council of 1945 see Orthodox Eastern Church, Russian, *Patriarkh Sergii i Ego Dukhovnoe Nasledstsvo,* pp. 321–27.

22. For the council of 1945 see Orthodox Eastern Church, Russian, *The Call of the Russian Church* (London: "The Soviet News," 1945).

23. Wassilij Alexeev, *Russian Orthodox Bishops in the Soviet Union, 1941–1953* (New York: Research Program on the USSR, 1954), p. 109.

IV. EMPIRE

1. Materials in this chapter are drawn chiefly from Wassilij Alexeev, *Russian Orthodox Bishops in the Soviet Union, 1941–1953* (New York: Research Program on the USSR, 1954), and *The Foreign Policy of the Moscow Patriarchate, 1939–1953* (New York: Research Program on the USSR, 1953).

Despite their pronounced point of view, these two works (in Russian) give excellent analyses of the relevant data. See also Orthodox Eastern Church, Russian, *Patriarkh Sergii i Ego Dukhovnoe Nasledstsvo* (*Patriarch Sergii and His Spiritual Legacy*) (Moscow: The Patriarchate, 1947), pp. 341–57.

2. Compare the broad hints that, because of the representatives of sister churches who were present, it was actually an ecumenical council; Orthodox Eastern Church, Russian, *op. cit.*, pp. 337–38.

3. See R. J. Fenno, Jr., ed., *The Yalta Conference* (Boston: D. C. Heath & Company, 1955). For Soviet foreign policy in the immediate postwar period see Hugh Seton-Watson, *From Lenin to Malenkov* (New York: Frederick A. Praeger, Inc., 1953).

4. For the Russian Orthodox position on seperation of church and state see William C. Fletcher, *A Study in Survival* (New York: The Macmillan Company, 1965), *passim*.

5. For the underground movement see Academy of Sciences of the USSR, *Sovremennoe Sektantstvo* (*Contemporary Sectarianism*) (Moscow: Academy Press, 1961), pp. 144–88.

6. See, e.g.: Stanley Evans, *Soviet Churches and the War* (London: Cobbett, 1943); William Howard Melish, *Religion Today in the USSR* (New York: National Council of American-Soviet Friendship, 1945).

7. Cf. Nikolai's statement in 1950, "It is easy to notice the huge similarity of the social truth of the new order of life to the moral understandings of Christianity, and in no wise possible to establish their bonds with the social activity of capitalism." (*Zhurnal Moskovskoi Patriarkhii*, August 1950).

8. Oleg Penkovsky is quoted as estimating that 60 percent of embassy personnel are intelligence officers (*The Penkovsky Papers* [London: William Collins Sons & Co., Ltd., 1965], p. 73). It should be noted that this work has been bitterly attacked as spurious by the Soviet Union. Thus it may be justly accused of having been extensively edited; however, as yet no convincing evidence that its data are false has been offered.

9. According to Penkovsky, "When a small delegation does not have among its members a GRU [Soviet military intelligence] officer, there must be a KGB [Ministry of State Security, the dominant branch of the Secret Police] officer or a KGB co-optee in it. No delegation ever goes abroad without some form of KGB involvement. . . . KGB officers travel with delegations even when it is hard to believe that there could be any intelligence officers in the delegation." *Ibid.*, p. 112.

10. This was a common accusation against Nikolai (cf. Judith Listowel, "The Red Rasputin," *Catholic World*, October

1953, pp. 43–48; "Is Soviet Youth Becoming Religious?" *ibid.*, November 1954, pp. 102–3).

11. Early in the history of the schism, the Living Church had secured partial recognition from the Ecumenical Patriarchate. Thus it may be possible, but not very likely, that he was included in the delegation in order to demonstrate to the other patriarchs that the schism had been healed.

12. U.S. Congress, Senate, Committee on the Judiciary, *Communist Controls on Religious Activity* (Washington, D.C.: U.S. Government Printing Office, 1959), pp. 14 and 15.

13. U.S. Congress, House, *The Kremlin's Espionage and Terror Organizations* (Washington, D.C.: U.S. Government Printing Office, 1959), p. 8. It is important to note that Deriabin here seems to be using the term "agent" to indicate one who cooperates in one capacity or another with the KGB, rather than in the sense of someone in the employment of and contractually or vocationally bound to the organization.

14. Orthodox Eastern Church, Russian, *op. cit.*, p. 362.

15. Simon Wolin and Robert M. Slusser, eds., *The Soviet Secret Police* (New York: Frederick A. Praeger, Inc., 1957), p. 193; cf. Alexander Solzhenitsyn, *One Day in the Life of Ivan Denisovich* (New York: Time, Inc., 1963).

16. See: Eugene Lyons, *Our Secret Allies* (New York: Duell, Sloan and Pearce, 1953); Boris Shub, *The Choice* (New York: Duell, Sloan and Pearce, 1950).

17. See Nicholas Zernov, *The Russian Religious Renaissance of the Twentieth Century* (London: Darton, Longman and Todd, 1963).

18. Absent were the Patriarchs of Jerusalem and Alexandria, while the Ecumenical Patriarch and the Greek representatives attended the jubilee celebrations only.

19. Cf. Orthodox Eastern Church, Russian, *Patriarkh Sergii i Ego Dukhovnoe Nasledstvo*, pp. 337–38.

20. See *Deiannia Soveshchannia Glav i Predstavitelei Aftokefal'nykh Pravoslavnykh Tserkvei v sviazi s Prazdnovaniem 500 Letiia Aftokefalii Russkoi Pravoslavnoi Tserkvi* (*Acts of the Conference of Heads and Representatives of the Autocephalous Orthodox Churches in Connection with the 500th Anniversary of the Autocephality of the Russian Orthodox Church*) (Moscow: The Patriarchate, 1949). Much of this work is available in English translation under the same (translated) title reproduced in limited-manuscript edition in Paris by the YMCA Press, 1952. Compare descriptions to be found in Matthew Spinka, *The Church in Soviet Russia* (New York: Oxford University Press, 1956) and in Wassilij Alexeev, *The Foreign Policy of the Moscow Patriarchate, 1939–1953*.

V. THE PASTOR: SIN AND THE CHRISTIAN LIFE

1. One of the best attempts at communicating this mystical aspect of Orthodoxy is Ruth Korper, *Candlelight Kingdom* (New York: The Macmillan Company, 1955). Further insight may be gained in George P. Fedotov, ed., *A Treasury of Russian Spirituality* (New York: Sheed and Ward, 1948), pp. 280–348.

2. Dmitrii V. Konstantinov, *Pravoslavnaia Molodezh' v Bor'be za Tserkov' v SSSR (Russian Orthodox Youth in the Struggle for the Church in the USSR)* (Munich: Institute for the Study of the USSR, 1956), *passim*.

3. That the majority of churchgoers are elderly has been widely and frequently reported; see, for example, I. D. Pantskhav, ed., *O Nekotorykh Osobennostiakh Sovremennoi Religioznoi Ideologii (Certain Peculiarities of Contemporary Religious Ideology)* (Moscow: Moscow University Press, 1964), p. 7. Walter Kolarz quotes Pariiskii, of the Leningrad Academy, as remarking, ". . . all those so-called 'grandmothers'—who must be immortal, by the way, since we've been hearing about them for the past forty years." (*Religion in the Soviet Union* [New York: St. Martin's Press, 1962], p. 148).

4. *Zhurnal Moskovskoi Patriarkhii (Journal of the Moscow Patriarchate*, hereafter cited as *ZMP*), March 1946 (reprinted in Nikolai, Metropolitan of Kolomna, *Slova, Rechi, Poslaniia, 1941–1946 gg.* [*Words, Speeches, Epistles, 1941–1946*, hereafter cited as *Slova* . . .] [Moscow: The Patriarchate, 1947], pp. 73–74).

5. *ZMP*, May 1946 (*Slova* . . ., p. 89).

6. *ZMP*, July 1945 (*Slova* . . ., pp. 36–37).

7. *ZMP*, June 1946 (*Slova* . . ., p. 96).

8. *ZMP*, May 1947 (*Slova* . . ., pp. 167–68).

9. *ZMP*, April 1947 (*Slova* . . ., pp. 163–65).

10. *ZMP*, April 1946 (*Slova* . . ., p. 77).

11. *ZMP*, May 1946 (*Slova* . . ., pp. 88–89).

12. *ZMP*, January 1945 (*Slova* . . ., pp. 23–25).

VI. THE PROPAGANDA

1. A. Veshchikov, "Milestones of a Great Journey," *Nauka i Religiia*, November 1962, p. 60, translation in *Religion in Communist Dominated Areas*, December 24, 1962, p. 8.

2. See Wassilij Alexeev, *Russian Orthodox Bishops in the Soviet Union, 1941–1953* (New York: Research Program on the USSR, 1954).

3. Thus, the first wave of arrests and closing of churches coincided with the civil war period. The forcible collectivization of the peasantry was accompanied by a bitter attack on the

churches, and the Great Purges caught up many churchmen
as well as Party members. The exception would seem to be
the rather stern attack on the Russian Orthodox patriarchate
in 1922–23, when the population at large was enjoying the
relative relaxation of the NEP period. However, this was
primarily a period of tension for the leadership of the Orthodox church, and those not involved in the patriarchate's
struggle against the Living Church were little affected.

4. This may be discerned in Academy of Sciences of the USSR,
   Sovremennoe Sektantstvo (Contemporary Sectarianism) (Mos-
   cow: Academy Press, 1961), pp. 144–88.

5. Marshall D. Shulman, *Stalin's Foreign Policy Reappraised* (New
   York: Atheneum, 1965), p. 81.

6. *Zhurnal Moskovskoi Patriarkhii (Journal of the Moscow Pa-*
   triarchate, hereafter cited as *ZMP*), September 1949 (reprinted
   in Nikolai, *We Will Defend Peace!* [hereafter cited as
   WWDP] [Moscow: The Patriarchate, 1952], pp. 16–24).

7. *ZMP,* August 1950 (*WWDP,* p. 40).

8. *ZMP,* September 1954 (reprinted in Nikolai, *Za Mir* [For
   Peace] [Moscow: The Patriarchate, 1955], p. 94).

9. *ZMP,* January 1953 (*Za Mir,* p. 27).

10. *In Defense of Peace,* No. 7, 1951 (*WWDP,* pp. 117–18).

11. *ZMP,* December 1953 (*Za Mir,* p. 56).

12. *ZMP,* September 1949 (*WWDP,* pp. 21–22).

13. *ZMP,* December 1953 (*Za Mir,* pp. 56–57).

14. *ZMP,* November 1950 (*WWDP,* pp. 47–48).

15. *ZMP,* July 1954 (*Za Mir,* pp. 70–71).

16. *ZMP,* January 1953 (*Za Mir,* pp. 24–27).

17. *ZMP,* December 1950 (*WWDP,* p. 57).

18. *ZMP,* March 1951 (*WWDP,* p. 75). It should be noted that this
    paragraph follows immediately after the Korean atrocities pas-
    sage quoted below.

19. *Za Mir,* p. 135.

20. Lenin's concept of Truth was much more practical in that he
    tended to subordinate truth to effectiveness: "For a material-
    ist, the 'success' of human practice proves the correspondence
    of our representations to the objective nature of the things we
    perceive." (V. I. Lenin, *Materialism and Empirio-Criticism*
    [New York International Publishers, 1934], p. 111).

21. For the beginnings of the international peace movement see:
    Shulman, *op. cit.,* pp. 80–91; Iain Phelps-Fetherston, *Soviet*
    International Front Organizations (New York: Frederick A.
    Praeger, Inc., 1965), p. 10.

22. Orthodox Eastern Church, Russian, *Conference in Defence of*
    Peace of All Churches and Religious Associations in the
    USSR (Moscow: The Patriarchate, 1952), pp. 38–40.

23. Shulman, *op. cit.*, pp. 136–37.
24. *Ibid.*, p. 87.
25. *Ibid.*, p. 246.
26. Orthodox Eastern Church, Russian, *loc. cit.*
27. ZMP, July 1954 (*Za Mir*, pp. 71–72).
28. ZMP, September 1954 (*Za Mir*, pp. 95–96).
29. *WWDP*, p. 49.
30. ZMP, March 1951 (*WWDP*, pp. 69–75).
31. Orthodox Eastern Church, Russian, *op. cit.*, pp. 88–89.
32. ZMP, September 1954 (*Za Mir*, pp. 94–95).
33. ZMP, July 1950 (*WWDP*, pp. 34–35).
34. See, e.g., M. Sheinman, "Tserkov' v SSSR i Kapitalisticheskoe Okruzhenie" ("The Church in the USSR and Capitalist Encirclement"), *Komsomol'skaia Pravda*, June 9, 1937, p. 3.
35. It should be noted here that the first official action of the Russion Orthodox patriarch after the accession to power of the Communists was to excommunicate them. This excommunication by the Orthodox church has yet to be lifted.
36. ZMP, September 1949 (*WWDP*, pp. 20–21).
37. This in fact did take place in the years immediately preceding and following Nikolai's death.
38. See Shulman, *op. cit.*, p. 188.
39. *WWDP*, pp. 107–8.
40. See ZMP, December 1950 (*WWDP*, pp. 58–59).
41. ZMP, August 1952 (*Za Mir*, p. 12).
42. ZMP, January 1953 (*Za Mir*, p. 31).
43. *Za Mir*, pp. 162–63.
44. ZMP, April 1952 (*WWDP*, p. 100).

VII. THE PASTOR: DEATH AND LIFE BEYOND

1. For the legal position of the church see William C. Fletcher, *A Study in Survival* (New York: The Macmillan Company, 1965), pp. 59–63. It should not be inferred that the churches are unable to find ways of circumventing these laws (cf. *ibid.*, pp. 63–69, 84–96). However, these activities do remain outside the law and are technically (and often actually) punishable.
2. There have been occasional complaints in the antireligious press that some pastors are preaching much more relevant sermons than is the norm, presenting able arguments to counter the antireligious propaganda. However, such pastors do so at their own risk, and a number have been arrested when their sermons attracted too much attention. See: "The Russian Orthodox Church and the Soviet Leadership," *Soviet Affairs Analysis Service*, No. 17 (1961–62), pp. 1–7; *Time*, February 16, 1962, pp. 26–27; and T. E. Bird, "Party, the Patriarch, and the World Council," *Commonweal*, April 13, 1962, p. 57.

3. Cf. Marcus Bach, *God and the Soviets* (New York: The Crowell-Collier Publishing Company, 1958), p. 158.
4. See, e.g.: V. A. Bliumkin, *Chest', Dostoinstvo, Gordost'* (*Honor, Worth, Pride*) (Moscow: "Knowledge" Press, 1963); P. Egides, *Smysl Zhizni—v Chem On?* (*The Meaning of Life—Where Is It?*) (Moscow: Political Literature Press, 1963); Society for the Dissemination of Political and Scientific Knowledge of the RSFSR, *O Kommunisticheskoi Etike* (*Communist Ethics*) (Leningrad: State Publishing House, 1962); and V. F. Sybkovets, *Ot Boga li Nravstovennost'* (*Is Morality from God?*) (Moscow: State Publishing House for Political Literature, 1961).
5. See N. A. Il'in, *Nauka i Religiia o Zhizni i Smerti* (*Science and Religion on Life and Death*) (Moscow: State Publishing House for Political Literature, 1959), pp. 141–45 *et passim.*
6. *Zhurnal Moskovskoi Patriarkhii* (*Journal of the Moscow Patriarchate*, hereafter cited as *ZMP*), August 1950.
7. *ZMP*, March 1946.
8. *ZMP*, December 1944.
9. See, e.g., A. A. Osipov, "Holy Scriptures," in H. M. Waddams, ed., *The Anglo-Russian Theological Conference, Moscow, July, 1956* (London: Faith Press, 1957).
10. See: D. Konstantinov, "Soundings in Unfamiliar Waters," *Bulletin of the Institute for the Study of the USSR*, May 1962, p. 39; Constantin de Grunwald, *The Churches and the Soviet Union* (New York: The Macmillan Company, 1962), pp. 19–20; and V. S. Ovchinnikov, "The Foundations of Scientific Atheism in the Technical Schools," *Voprosy Filosofii*, July 1961, pp. 143–44.
11. See: Nicholas Zernov, *Eastern Christendom* (London: Faith Press, 1961); A. Shmeman, *Istoricheskii Put' Pravoslaviia* (*The Historical Way of Orthodoxy*) (New York: Chekhov Press, 1954).
12. Cf. Iosif A. Kryvelev, *Kniga o Biblii* (*A Book on the Bible*) (Moscow: State Publishing House for Social and Economic Literature, 1958); G. Livshits, *Chto Takoe "Sviashchennye Knigi?"* (*What Are the "Holy Books?"*) (Minsk: Ministry of Education of the Belorussian SSR, 1962).
13. See Academy of Sciences of the USSR, *Sovremennoe Sektantstvo* (*Contemporary Sectarianism*) (Moscow: Academy Press, 1961), pp. 144–88.
14. Academy of Sciences of the USSR, *Voprosy Istorii Religii i Ateizma* (*Problems of the History of Religion and Atheism*) (Moscow: Académy Press, 1962), IX, pp. 166–67.
15. These references are conveniently compiled in Nadezhda Teodorovich, "The Catacomb Church in the USSR," *Bulletin*

of the Institute for the Study of the USSR, April 1965, pp. 3–14.

16. *ZMP,* September 1946.
17. "Idealistic" is here used not as a philosophical technical term referring to a theory of mind or spirit as opposed to materialism, but in the more prosaic sense of one who idealizes: a visionary, a dreamer.
18. This is best illustrated in his fable of the Grand Inquisitor in *The Brothers Karamazov;* cf. *Summer Notes on Winter Impressions* and *Diary of a Writer.*
19. *ZMP,* August 1946.
20. *ZMP,* December 1945.
21. *ZMP,* February 1946.
22. *ZMP,* November 1944.

VIII. THE NEW ERA

1. For the troubled times surrounding Stalin's death see: H. Schwartz, *The Red Phoenix: Russia Since World War II* (New York: Frederick A. Praeger, Inc., 1961); E. Crankshaw, *Russia Without Stalin* (New York: The Viking Press, Inc., 1956); and "Monitor," *The Death of Stalin* (London: Wingate, 1958).
2. As a case in point, it is interesting that the postwar *détente* was considered one of the mistakes of the "personality cult," and the reversion to the policies of the earlier Stalin was undertaken in the name of de-Stalinization in the 1960s. See *Nauka i Religiia,* April 1962, pp. 48–49.
3. For Karpov's dual role see: U.S. Congress, Senate, Committee on the Judiciary, *Communist Controls on Religious Activity* (Washington, D.C.: U.S. Government Printing Office, 1959), pp. 2, 5–8; Vladimir and Evdokia Petrov, *Empire of Fear* (New York: Frederick A. Praeger, Inc., 1956), p. 97; Frederick Barghoorn, *Soviet Russian Nationalism* (New York: Oxford University Press, 1956), p. 313; Simon Wolin and Robert M. Slusser, eds., *The Soviet Secret Police* (New York: Frederick A. Praeger, Inc., 1957), pp. 23–24; David J. Dallin, *The Changing World of Soviet Russia* (New Haven, Conn.: Yale University Press, 1956); and Walter Kolarz, *Religion in the Soviet Union* (New York: St. Martin's Press, 1962), p. 54.
4. One of the worst errors of this sort was committed by the (Karlovtsi) Synod Abroad, when, during the famine of 1921–22, it attempted to persuade the West to undertake renewed armed intervention in Russia, thereby providing the Soviet state with the proof it needed that the church's resistance to confiscation of its valuables to aid the suffering was counterrevolutionary. See: William C. Emhardt, *Religion in*

Soviet Russia (London: Morehouse, 1929), pp. 242–50; Sergii
V. Troitskii, *O Nepravde Karlovatskogo Raskola* (*On the
Falsity of the Karlovtsi Schism*) (Paris: Editions de l'Exarchat
Patriarchal Russe en Europe Occidentale, 1960), p. 24.

5. Hélène and Pierre Lazareff, *The Soviet Union after Stalin*
(London: Odhams Press, 1955), p. 202.

6. *Pravda*, November 11, 1954.

7. In 1937, for example, he had publicly supported the antireligious campaign in the Ukraine (F. Oleshchuk, "Bor'ba
Bol'shevistskoi Partii protiv Religii" ["The Struggle of the
Bolshevik Party against Religion"] *Antireligioznik*, October
1937, p. 15). For the decree as part of Khrushchev's struggle
for power see G. D. Embree, *The Soviet Union Between the
19th and 20th Party Congresses, 1952–1956* (The Hague: Martinus Nijhoff, 1959), pp. 106–7.

8. Nathaniel Davis, "Religion and Communist Government in the
Soviet Union and Eastern Europe" (unpublished Ph.D. dissertation, Fletcher School of Law and Diplomacy, 1960), p.
314.

9. See: E. C. Parker, "East-West Ecumenical Contacts," *Christian
Century*, October 30, 1962, p. 1187; Aleksandr A. Bogolepov,
Tserkov' pod Vlast'iu Kommunizma (*The Church under the
Rule of Communism*) (Munich: Institute for the Study of the
USSR, 1958), p. 53; George C. Guins, *Communism on the
Decline* (The Hague: Martinus Nijhoff, 1956), p. 255.

10. See George Gibian, *Interval of Freedom: Soviet Literature
During the Thaw, 1954–1957* (Minneapolis: University of
Minneapolis Press, 1960).

11. See *Ezhegodnik Knigi SSSR* (*Yearbook of Books of the USSR*)
(Moscow: All-Union Book Press, 1955 and 1956).

12. See, e.g., Alexander Solzhenitsyn, *One Day in the Life of Ivan
Denisovich* (New York: Time, Inc., 1963), pp. ix–x.

13. David J. Dallin and Boris I. Nicolaevsky, *Forced Labour in
Soviet Russia* (New Haven, Conn.: Yale University Press,
1947).

14. Victor Tchernavin, *I Speak for the Silent* (New York: Hale,
Cushman and Flint, 1935).

15. *Out of the Deep: Letters from Soviet Timber Camps* (London:
Bles, 1933).

16. Joseph Scholmer, *Vorkuta* (New York: Holt, Rinehart and
Winston, Inc., 1955).

17. See William C. Fletcher, *A Study in Survival* (New York: The
Macmillan Company, 1965), pp. 91–92, 149.

18. Compare the statement by the Hungarian author Tamas Aczel
in a speech delivered in Stockholm on February 9, 1959: "The
last blow fell when Nagy let the prisoners out of the con-

centration camps. We had to face these former prisoners and we also had to face ourselves. I will never forget the night I and a few others spent with our friends Haraszty and Geza Losonczy. We began talking at 6 P.M. on an evening and finished at 9 A.M. the next morning. After that we were Communists no longer." (Radio Free Europe news release, Item No. 721/59).

19. Cf. Richard Crossman, ed., *The God that Failed* (New York: Harper & Row, Publishers, 1950).

20. See: *New Leader*, July 16, 1956; Bertram D. Wolfe, *Khrushchev and Stalin's Ghost* (New York: Frederick A. Praeger, Inc., 1957); and *The Anti-Stalin Campaign and International Communism* (New York: Columbia University Press, 1956).

21. For example, in the discussion about re-establishing the patriarchate in 1917, a peasant argued, "We have a tsar no more; no father, whom we may love. It is impossible to love a synod, and therefore we, the peasants, want a Patriarch." Grigorii N. Trubetskoi, *Krasnaia Rossiia i Sviataia Rus'* (*Red Russia and Holy Rus*) (Paris: YMCA Press, 1947), pp. 305–6.

22. Cf. Elinor Lipper, *Eleven Years in Soviet Prison Camps* (London: Hollis and Carter, 1950), pp. 142–43.

23. For background to the ecumenical interest in Russia I am indebted to Dr. Roswell P. Barnes.

24. For descriptions of the confrontation see *The New York Times*, March 18, 1956, p. 27.

25. *Translation of Extracts from Articles Published in Journal of the Moscow Patriarchate* (n.p., n.p., n.d.).

26. *Ibid.*, pp. 32–33. See Chapter VI.

27. Nikolai repeated this answer when asked about the germ warfare campaign by reporters on his subsequent visit to the U.S. *The New York Times*, June 3, 1956, p. 3.

28. For Western opinions on the change in Nikolai's attitude see, e.g., I. Swan, "The Disappearance of Metropolitan Nikolai," *Bulletin of the Institute for the Study of the USSR*, May 1961, pp. 49–50.

29. See George Mikes, *The Hungarian Revolution* (London: Andre Deutsch, 1957).

30. *The New York Times*, November 26, 1956, p. 14.

31. W. A. Visser 't'Hooft, ed., *The First Assembly of the World Council of Churches* (New York: Harper & Row, Publishers, 1949), p. 30.

32. *The New York Times*, August 10, 1958, p. 10.

33. *Ibid.*, August 24, 1959, p. 3.

34. See Swan, *loc. cit.*

35. *The New York Times*, June 4, 1956.

36. *Zhurnal Moskovskoi Patriarkhii* (*Journal of the Moscow Patriarchate*), January 1957.

IX. THE PASTOR: PATRIOTISM AND MARTYRDOM

1. Orthodox Eastern Church, Russian, *Pravda o Religii v Rossiia* (Moscow: The Patriarchate, 1952), pp. 51–52.
2. *Zhurnal Moskovskoi Patriarkhii* (*Journal of the Moscow Patriarchate*, hereafter cited as ZMP), March 1947.
3. ZMP, January 1946.
4. ZMP, July 1946 (reprinted in Nikolai, Metropolitan of Kolomna, *Slova, Rechi, Poslaniia, 1941–1946 gg.* [*Words, Speeches, Epistles, 1941–1946*, hereafter cited as *Slova* . . .] [Moscow: The Patriarchate, 1947], pp. 100–1). The Tatars were Asiatic invaders who occupied Russia for two centuries. The victory of Dmitrii Donskoi over the Tatars in 1380 marked the beginning of the decline and eventual disruption of Tatar rule.
5. *Ibid.*
6. See Iain Phelps-Fetherston, *Soviet International Front Organizations* (New York: Frederick A. Praeger, Inc., 1965), pp. 22–27.
7. See G. P. Fedotov, *The Russian Religious Mind* (New York: Harper & Row, Publishers, 1960), pp. 94–110.
8. ZMP, August 1946 (*Slova* . . ., p. 105).
9. ZMP, October 1946.
10. ZMP, *June* 1946.
11. ZMP, March 1946.
12. ZMP, August 1946 (*Slova* . . ., p. 103).

X. THE BREAK

1. See his "Holy Scriptures," in H. M. Waddams, ed., *The Anglo-Russian Theological Conference, Moscow, July, 1956* (London: Faith Press, 1957).
2. This possibility is given added credence when one considers the state interest in the theological schools. See: Walter Kolarz, *Religion in the Soviet Union* (New York: St. Martin's Press, 1962), p. 91; Dmitrii V. Konstantinov, *Pravoslavnaia Molodezh' v Bor'be za Tserkov' v SSSR* (*Russian Orthodox Youth in the Struggle for the Church in the USSR*) (Munich: Institute for the Study of the USSR, 1956), p. 54.
3. For examples of the theme of corrupt clergy in antireligious propaganda see: Academy of Sciences of the USSR, *Uspekhi Sovremennoi Nauki i Religiia* (*Contemporary Science's Success and Religion*) (Moscow: Academy Press, 1961), pp. 19–20; *Nauka i Religiia*, July 1963, p. 92; *Vecherniaia Moskva*, May 14, 1964; P. Darmanskii, *Pobeg iz T'my* (*Flight from Darkness*) (Moscow: "Sovetskaia Rossiia" Press, 1961), pp.

30–61; *Komsomol'skaia Pravda,* March 22, 1964; I. D. Pant-skhav, ed., *O Nekotorykh Osobennostiakh Sovremennoi Religioznoi Ideologii (Certain Peculiarities of Contemporary Religious Ideology)* (Moscow: Moscow University Press, 1964), p, 205; and the summary in Kolarz, *op. cit.,* pp. 86–94.

4. *Pravda,* December 6, 1959. Osipov's story, as he himself relates it, seems perfectly credible, except for the difficult question of why he would have compounded his difficulties with the church by marrying his second wife in civil ceremony. Such registration of marriage would do nothing whatsoever to purge the relationship of its sinful character in the eyes of the church, nor would it do much to mitigate the irregularity of the relationship in the eyes of society. Inasmuch as priests are outside the secular social security system, the civil ceremony would be irrelevant to providing for the wife's security in the event of Osipov's death or inability to produce income. It would seem that such an action could only have been motivated by a desire to embarrass the church (while an illicit relationship would place Osipov under personal interdiction, it need not create great embarrassment for the church provided it were handled with discretion). Osipov's indiscretion could not be kept secret after the civil registration of marriage, however, and thus one can only wonder whether or not Osipov's action in this case were not a calculated attempt to do damage to the church. If this be the case, then Osipov's claim that at that time he was in doubt about, but not yet hostile to, the church may be suspect.

5. See, e.g.: Simon Wolin and Robert M. Slusser, eds., *The Soviet Secret Police* (New York: Frederick A. Praeger, Inc., 1957), pp. 215, 335; U.S. Congress, House, *Patterns of Communist Espionage* (Washington, D.C.: U.S. Government Printing Office, 1959), pp. 60–65.

6. *Zhurnal Moskovskoi Patriarkhii (Journal of the Moscow Patriarchate,* hereafter cited as *ZMP*), February 1960.

7. *ZMP,* March 1960.

8. I. Swan, "The Disappearance of Metropolitan Nikolai," *Bulletin of the Institute for the Study of the USSR,* May 1961, pp. 46–47.

9. *ZMP,* April 1960.

10. *Ibid.*

11. Nadezhda Teodorovich, "Increasing Pressure on the Moscow Patriarchate," *Bulletin of the Institute for the Study of the USSR,* October 1962, p. 43.

12. Swan, *loc. cit.*

13. *Pravda, April 6,* 1960; *The New York Times,* April 6, 1960.

14. Michael Bourdeaux, *Opium of the People* (London: Faber and Faber, Ltd., 1965), pp. 80–81.
15. *ZMP*, June 1960.
16. *ZMP*, May 1960.
17. *ZMP*, July 1960.
18. *ZMP*, October 1960.
19. Swan, *loc. cit.*
20. Dmitrii Konstantinov, "A Turning Point in the Moscow Patriarchate's Policy," *Bulletin of the Institute for the Study of the USSR*, March 1963, p. 21.
21. I am indebted to Dr. Paul B. Anderson for some material on Nikolai's hospitalization and death.
22. Nikita Struve, *Les Chretiens en U.R.S.S.* (Paris: Editions du Seuil, 1963), pp. 271–74.
23. Swan, *loc. cit.*
24. *ZMP*, January 1962.
25. K. Fotiev, "K Konchine Mitropolita Nikolaia" ("The Death of Metropolitan Nikolai"), *Posev*, January 29, 1961, p. 7.

Bibliography

Academy of Sciences of the USSR. *Sovremennoe Sektantstvo (Contemporary Sectarianism)*. Moscow, Academy Press, 1961.
—— *Uspekhi Sovremennoi Nauki i Religiia (Contemporary Science's Success and Religion)*. Moscow, Academy Press, 1961.
—— *Voprosy Istorii Religii i Ateizma (Problems of the History of Religion and Atheism)*. Moscow, Academy Press, 1962.
Alexeev, Wassilij. *The Foreign Policy of the Moscow Patriarchate, 1939–1953*. New York, Research Program on the USSR, 1953.
—— *Russian Orthodox Bishops in the Soviet Union, 1941–1953*. New York, Research Program on the USSR, 1954.
American Committee for Liberation. *The Beleaguered Fortress*. New York, Information Center on Soviet Affairs, 1963.
Bach, Marcus. *God and the Soviets*. New York, The Crowell-Collier Publishing Company, 1958.
Barghoorn, Frederick. *Soviet Russian Nationalism*. New York, Oxford University Press, 1956.
Bliumkin, V. A. *Chest', Dostoinstvo, Gordost' (Honor, Worth, Pride)*. Moscow, Knowledge Press, 1963.
Bogolepov, Aleksandr A. *Tserkov' pod Vlast'iu Kommunizma (The Church under the Rule of Communism)*. Munich, Institute for the Study of the USSR, 1958.
Bourdeaux, Michael. *Opium of the People*. London, Faber and Faber, Ltd., 1965.
Comité d'Information sur la Situation des Chrétiens en Union Soviétique (*Situation des Chrétiens en Union Soviétique*), Paris, n.p., 1965.
Crankshaw, E. *Russia Without Stalin*. New York, The Viking Press, Inc., 1956.
Crossman, Richard, ed. *The God That Failed*. New York, Harper & Row, Publishers, 1950.
Curtiss, John Shelton. *The Russian Church and the Soviet State, 1917–1950*. Boston, Little, Brown and Company, 1953.
Dallin, David J. *The Changing World of Soviet Russia*. New Haven, Conn., Yale University Press, 1956.
—— and Nicolaevsky, Boris I. *Forced Labour in Soviet Russia*. New Haven, Conn., Yale University Press, 1947.
Darmanskii, P. *Pobeg iz T'my (Flight from Darkness)*. Moscow, Sovetskaia Rossiia Press, 1861.
Davis, Nathaniel. "Religion and Communist Government in the So-

viet Union and Eastern Europe" (unpublished Ph.D. dissertation, Fletcher School of Law and Diplomacy, 1960).

Deiannia Soveshchannia Glav i Predstavitelei Aftokefal'nykh Pravoslavnykh Tserkvei v svaizi s Prazdnovaniem 500 Letiia Aftokefalii Russkoi Pravoslavnoi Tserkvi (Acts of the Conference of Heads and Representatives of the Autocephalous Orthodox Churches in Connection with the 500th Anniversary of the Autocephality of the Russian Orthodox Church). Moscow, The Patriarchate, 1949.

Dinerstein, Herbert S. and Gouré, Leon. *Two Studies in Soviet Controls.* Glencoe, Ill., Free Press of Glencoe, 1955.

Egides, P. *Smysl Zhizni—v Chem On? (The Meaning of Life—Where Is It?).* Moscow, Political Literature Press, 1963.

Embree, G. D. *The Soviet Union Between the 19th and 20th Party Congresses, 1952–1956.* The Hague, Martinus Nijhoff, 1959.

Emhardt, William C. *Religion in Soviet Russia.* London, Morehouse, 1929.

Evans, Stanley George. *The Russian Church Today.* London; Zeno Publishers, 1955.

—— *Soviet Churches and the War.* London, Cobbett, 1943.

Fedotov, G. P. *The Russian Religious Mind.* New York, Harper & Row, Publishers, 1960.

—— *A Treasury of Russian Spirituality.* New York, Sheed and Ward, 1948.

Fenno, Jr., R. J., ed. *The Yalta Conference.* Boston, D. C. Heath & Company, 1955.

Fletcher, William C. *A Study in Survival.* New York, The Macmillan Company, 1965.

Gibian, George. *Interval of Freedom: Soviet Liturature During the Thaw, 1954–1957.* Minneapolis, University of Minneapolis Press, 1960.

Gidulianov, P. V. *Otdelenie Tserkvi ot Gosudarstva (Separation of Church from State).* Moscow, State Publishing House for Juridical Literature, 1929.

de Grunwald, Constantin. *The Churches and the Soviet Union.* New York, The Macmillan Company, 1962.

Guins, George C. *Communism on the Decline.* The Hague, Martinus Nijhoff, 1956.

Iaroslavskii, E. *O Religii (On Religion).* Moscow, State Publishing House for Political Literature, 1957.

Il'in, N. A. *Nauka i Religiia o Zhizni i Smerti (Science and Religion on Life and Death).* Moscow, State Publishing House for Political Literature, 1959.

Iwanow, Boris, ed. *Religion in the USSR.* Munich, Institute for the Study of the USSR, 1960.

Kolarz, Walter. *Religion in the Soviet Union.* New York, St. Martin's Press, 1962.

Konstantinov, Dmitrii V. *Pravoslavnaia Molodezh' v Bor'be za Tserkov' v SSSR (Russian Orthodox Youth in the Struggle for the Church in the USSR).* Munich, Institute for the Study of the USSR, 1956.

Korper, Ruth. *Candlelight Kingdom.* New York, The Macmillan Company, 1955.

Kryvelev, Iosif A. *Kniga o Biblii (A Book on the Bible).* Moscow, State Publishing House for Social and Economic Literature, 1958.

Lazareff, Hélène and Pierre. *The Soviet Union after Stalin.* London, Odhams Press, 1955.

Lenin, V. I. *Materialism and Empirio-Criticism.* New York International Publishers, 1934.

Lipper, Elinor. *Eleven Years in Soviet Prison Camps.* London, Hollis and Carter, 1950.

Livshits, G. *Chto Takoe "Sviashchennye Knigi?" (What Are the "Holy Books"?).* Minsk, Ministry of Education of the Belorussian SSR, 1962.

Lyons, Eugene. *Our Secret Allies.* New York, Duell, Sloan and Pearce, 1953.

Melish, William Howard. *Religion Today in the USSR.* New York, National Council of American-Soviet Friendship, 1945.

Mikes, George. *The Hungarian Revolution.* London, Andre Deutsch, 1957.

"Monitor." *The Death of Stalin.* London, Wingate, 1958.

Nikolai, Metropolitan of Kolomna. *Slova, Rechi, Poslaniia, 1941–1946 gg. (Words, Speeches, Epistles, 1941–1946).* Moscow, The Patriarchate, 1947.

—— *We Will Defend Peace!* Moscow, The Patriarchate, 1952.

—— *Za Mir (For Peace).* Moscow, The Patriarchate, 1955.

Orthodox Eastern Church, Russian. *The Call of the Russian Church.* London, The Soviet News, 1945.

—— *Conference in Defence of Peace of All Churches and Religious Associations in the USSR.* Moscow, The Patriarchate, 1952.

—— *Patriarkh Sergii i Ego Dukhovnoe Nasledstsvo (Patriarch Sergii and His Spiritual Legacy).* Moscow, The Patriarchate, 1947.

—— *The Russian Orthodox Church, Organization, Situation, Activity.* Moscow, The Patriarchate, 1959.

—— *The Truth about Religion in Russia.* Authorized translation by E. N. C. Sergeant of *Pravda o Religii v Rossiia.* New York, Hutchinson, 1944.

Out of the Deep: Letters from Soviet Timber Camps. London, Bles, 1933.

Pantskhav, I. D., ed. *O Nekotorykh Osobennostiakh Sovremennoi Religioznoi Ideologii (Certain Peculiarities of Contemporary Religious Ideology).* Moscow, Moscow University Press, 1964.

Penkovsky, Oleg. *The Penkovsky Papers.* London, William Collins Sons & Co., Ltd., 1965.

Petrov, Vladimir and Evdokia. *Empire of Fear.* New York, Frederick A. Praeger, Inc., 1956.

Phelps-Fetherston, Iain. *Soviet International Front Organizations.* New York, Frederick A. Praeger, Inc., 1965.

Pol'skii, Mikhail. *Kanonicheskoe Polozhenie Vysshei Tserkovnoi Vlasti v S.S.S.R. i Zagranitsei (The Canonical Position of the Highest Church Authority in the USSR and Abroad).* Jordanville, N.Y., Iov Pochaevskii Press in the Holy Trinity Monastery, 1948.

Shmeman, A. *Istoricheskii Put' Pravoslaviia (The Historical Way of Orthodoxy).* New York, Chekhov Press, 1954.

Scholmer, Joseph. *Vorkuta.* New York, Holt, Rinehart and Winston, Inc., 1955.

Schwartz, H. *The Red Phoenix: Russia Since World War II.* New York, Frederick A. Praeger, Inc., 1961.

Seton-Watson, Hugh. *From Lenin to Malenkov.* New York, Frederick A. Praeger, Inc., 1953.

Shub, Boris. *The Choice.* New York, Duell, Sloan and Pearce, 1950.

Shulman, Marshall D. *Stalin's Foreign Policy Reappraised.* New York, Atheneum, 1965.

Society for the Dissemination of Political and Scientific Knowledge of the RSFSR. *O Kommunisticheskoi Etike (Communist Ethics).* Leningrad, State Publishing House, 1962.

Solzhenitsyn, Alexander. *One Day in the Life of Ivan Denisovich.* New York, Time, Inc. Book Division, 1963.

Spinka, Matthew. *The Church in Soviet Russia.* New York, Oxford University Press, 1956.

Struve, Nikita. *Les Chrétiens en U.R.S.S.* Paris, Editions du Seuil, 1963.

Sybkovets, V. F. *Ot Boga li Nravstvennost' (Is Morality from God?).* Moscow, State Publishing House for Political Literature, 1961.

Tchernavin, Victor. *I Speak for the Silent.* New York, Hale, Cushman and Flint, 1935.

Translation of Extracts from Articles Published in Journal of the Moscow Patriarchate, n.p., n.p. n.d.

Troitskii, Sergii V. *O Nepravde Karlovatskogo Raskola (On the Falsity of the Karlovtsi Schism).* Paris, Editions de l'Exarchat Patriarchal Russe en Europe Occidentale, 1960.

Trubetskoi, Grigorii N. *Krasnaia Rossiia i Sviataia Rus'* (*Red Russia and Holy Rus*). Paris, YMCA Press, 1947.

Ugolovnyi Kodeks RSFSR (*Criminal Code of the RSFSR*). Moscow, Juridical Literature Press, 1964.

U.S. Congress, House, *The Kremlin's Espionage and Terror Organizations*. Washington, D.C. U.S. Government Printing Office. 1959.

—— *Patterns of Communist Espionage*. Washington, D.C., U.S. Government Printing Office, 1959.

U.S. Congress, Senate, Committee on the Judiciary. *Communist Controls on Religious Activity*. Washington, D.C., U.S. Government Printing Office, 1959.

USSR. *Soviet War Documents*. Washington, D.C., Embassy of the USSR, 1943.

Visser t'Hooft, W. A., ed. *The First Assembly of the World Council of Churches*. New York, Harper & Row, Publishers, 1949.

Waddams, H. M., ed. *The Anglo-Russian Theological Conference, Moscow, July, 1956*. London, Faith Press, 1957.

Werth, Alexander. *Russia at War, 1941–1945*. New York, E. P. Dutton & Company, Inc., 1964.

Wittlin, Thaddeus. *Time Stopped at 6:30*. New York, The Bobbs-Merrill Co., Inc., 1965.

Wolfe, Bertram D. *Khrushchev and Stalin's Ghost*. New York, Frederick A. Praeger, Inc., 1957.

Wolin, Simon and Slusser, Robert M., eds. *The Soviet Secret Police*. New York, Frederick A. Praeger, Inc., 1957.

Yudin, N. I. *Pravda o Petersburgskikh "Sviatyniakh"* (*The Truth about the "Shrines" of St. Petersburg*). Leningrad, Lenin Press, 1962.

Zernov, Nicholas. *Eastern Christendom*. London, Faith Press, 1961.

—— *The Russian Religious Renaissance of the Twentieth Century*. London, Darton, Longman and Todd, 1963.

Index